CRISIS, CO-HABITATION, CONTRACEPTION & DI

FIVE SETS OF PROPOS
SYNOI

GW01606497

By Anthony E.C.W. Spencer

Russell-Spencer Ltd

Crisis, Co-habitation, Contraception and Divorce.
Five sets of proposals for the two Synods.

By Anthony E.C.W. Spencer

Copyright © Anthony E.C.W. Spencer

Published 2014 by Russell-Spencer Ltd.,
Stone House, Hele, Taunton, Somerset TA4 1AJ, England
sociorelresearch@btinternet.com

The right of Anthony Spencer to be identified as the author of this book has been asserted by him in accordance with the Copyright, Designs and Patents Act, 1988.

Printed by Sarsen Press, Winchester
Typesetting & distribution by Russell-Spencer Ltd

ISBN 978-1-905270-73-6

DEDICATION

To Rosemary Anne Spencer (neé Abson).

When asked at the age of four what she wanted to do when she was grown up, she answered:
'I want to look after a hundred babies'.
She looked after five of her own, with extraordinary love & care, and as a midwife she must have looked after many hundreds, and so well that other midwives asked her to deliver their own babies.

And to the thousands of

Latin Rite cardinals, archbishops and bishops of the Catholic Church

who have never had to get and hold a job to support a family, never courted and married a wife, never had to get up in the middle of the night to change the baby's nappy, never had to worry about their children's education, health and misdemeanours, their teenage tantrums, their choice of friends, their failure to achieve their ambitions, their difficulties in getting a job and progressing in a career, nor about their own personal marital difficulties, their own failures as Christian parents and husbands, and never had to cope in old age with wives who are sick or suffering from disabilities or dementia.

These middle-aged and elderly men, once themselves nurtured in the family of orientation – who have never fathered a child, but are often called the Fathers of the Church – are condemned by history to make decisions on behalf of the institutional church about the dilemmas of real fathers (and their wives), although they have no personal experience whatever of the family of procreation.
May God have mercy on them!
They know not what they do.

ACKNOWLEDGEMENTS

I am grateful to the editor of *Renew* for permission to quote extracts from articles by Benkert, Doyle, Lomas and Sipe,
to Robert Kaiser for permission to reproduce a footnote in his book *The Encyclical that Never Was*, to the editor of *The Irish Times* for permission to reproduce on the back cover some text published on 16 June, 2014, to Kevin Kelly for permission to quote a passage from his book *Divorce and Second Marriage* and to Crossroad for permission to publish quotations from Robert McClory's *Turning Point.* I am unable to acknowledge the kindness of the owners of the copyright of the English translations of two books (Schillebeeckx *Marriage. Secular Reality and Saving Mystery* and Georges Duby's *The Knight, the Lady and the Priest)* for their permission to quote passages from them, as persistent efforts to trace them have been unsuccessful.

I acknowledge the kindness of the Katholiek Sociaal-Kerkelijk Instituut which provided Mass attendance figures for the Netherlands, and that of the editor of the *Scottish Catholic Directory*, who provided them for Scotland.

Christopher Smart, Richard Spencer and Clare Harvey gave very useful IT advice.

Dr Michael Winter and Prof. Tina Beattie made helpful suggestions about documentary sources. Dr Rosemary Harris was kind enough to read an early draft of Chapter Five. For errors that remain I alone am responsible

Table of Contents

PREFACE

There must be many millions across the world who endorse the view expressed by Dr Mary McAleese, former President of the Irish Republic, summarised on the back cover of this book. I suspect that many of the leaders of Catholic Church Reform International (CCRI) did so, and still do. But they took the view that they should support Francis Bergoglio, the newly elected Bishop of Rome, in his attempt to grapple with the crisis in the Catholic Church by calling first an Extraordinary Synod on the Family in 2014, and then an Ordinary Synod in 2015. In February CCRI invited me to join an expert committee to prepare a CCRI paper to be submitted to the Synod.

. I prepared six papers in all for CCRI, and in re-arranged and edited form their substance is reproduced in this book. It struck me when drafting them that the issues that the two synods ought to be grappling with are more or less those that took the bishops at Vatican II four sessions, each of several months, only to find that their work was side-tracked once they had left Rome in 1966. Though, one must add, few of them demonstrated much moral courage in defending, after the Council, what they had done while it was in session.

The arrangement of this book is described in Chapter One, the Introduction. Each chapter is preceded by a summary. A wide range of issues connected with the family and human sexuality are deliberately excluded from this book. Only three have been selected, their background reviewed, and then a solution suggested. To underpin them a programme of preparation and support is set out in Chapter Five.

Any serious scholar studying the crisis described in Chapter One will ask: how did it happen? Effective societies and institutions have arrangements to monitor themselves and their environment. They develop conflict resolution systems. How did it happen that at the Renaissance, and in the mid-nineteenth century, these systems did not function? And when they did function in the early 1960s, how were they so quickly rendered ineffective? And what action should the institutional Church take to protect the faithful from a repetition? These issues, only indirectly related to the family, are considered in Chapter Six.

Jesus made much use of parables. So let this preface end with one. A mighty army once had a new commander-in-chief. He lived in a tiny enclave in Italy. His huge army had 1.214 billion soldiers, stationed all over the world, under the command of 5,132 senior officers and 413,418 junior officers. This new commander-in-chief was concerned about the lack of discipline in his army, and decided to summon a council of war.

However, there was a little problem. The ordinary soldiers – who used to call themselves 'the poor bloody infantry' – had great experience of warfare. But for many centuries the army had a strict rule, that no one could be commissioned if he had had any experience on the field of battle, and - once commissioned - no officer was allowed to engage in warfare. Field-marshals, generals and colonels were given magnificent uniforms. They reviewed their troops with great ceremony, accompanied by wonderful music. They were once able to maintain strict discipline, and impose the death sentence on hundreds of millions for misconduct on the field of battle, but now their troops were close to mutiny. So the new commander-in-chief summoned fifty of his most trusted field-marshals, generals and colonels to give him their advice.

In a far-away island in North-West Europe the former regimental sergeant-major –very clever and very experienced in warfare – used parade-ground language to describe the council of war. Meanwhile, a private soldier, far older than even the field-marshals, decided to write this book and reflect on his miserable military achievements. Of his five children, 100% had been baptised. Of his ten grandchildren, 50%, and of his (so far) four great-grandchildren, 25%. Out of his nineteen descendants, just one is found at Mass on a Sunday. He appreciated that the new commander-in-chief would never read this book, nor any of his field-marshals, generals and colonels. But perhaps some of the mutinous troops might find it interesting.

18.9.2014

CHAPTER ONE

ANOTHER CRISIS IN THE CATHOLIC CHURCH AND HOW IT CAME ABOUT.

SUMMARY

The current crisis over marriage, sexuality and the family had its origins in the encyclical of Pius XI, Casti Connubii in 1930. Its condemnations of all forms of contraception were modified in 1950 and 1952 by Pius XII, allowing use of the methods based on the 'safe period'. But around 1960 three developments focused public attention on the official condemnation of contraceptive practices. One was the development of 'the pill' as an effective means of contraception. Another was the summoning of Vatican II, and the third was the growing awareness among confessors of the practical difficulties of the Ogino-Knaus methods, and their impact on family life.

Cardinal Suenens advised Pope John XXIII to create a Pontifical Commission on Population, Family and Birth. It was set up in March, 1963, and first met in October. Paul VI revealed its existence in June, 1964, raising expectations of a change in the official position of the Church. The experts on the Commission were phased out in 1966, leaving the theologians to draft their conclusions and discuss them with the sixteen cardinals and bishops appointed to the Commission to approve the report and submit it to the Pope. Only one opposed the final draft, which was delivered to the Pope on 28 June, 1966.

The text of the report was leaked in April, 1967, and the conclusions of the Commission further raised expectations of a radical change in the official teaching of the Church. In August, 1968, the encyclical Humanae Vitae was published. Far from being 'received' it provoked uproar and anger that lasted until the end of 1969. Many secular and regular priests left the ministry. National Episcopal Conferences reacted in different ways, but none demanded an extraordinary synod to discuss the encyclical and the crisis it had provoked.

A number of books were written at the time about the Commission, its report and Humanae Vitae, and many more were published towards the end of the century. After the election of Pope John Paul II in 1978 it became clear that acceptance of the encyclical was the litmus test of suitability for episcopal ordination, and expressions of dissent among bishops were postponed until after their retirement.

The Roman Curia continued to backtrack on Vatican II, and the CDF continued to persecute theologians who expressed dissenting views. There were very evident problems within the Curia, but the latter, the faithful (the People of God) and the secular world were taken by surprise when Benedict Ratzinger resigned. They were even more surprised when the cardinals elected to the See of Rome a Latin American Jesuit, who has kept on surprising them.

Francis Bergoglio's biggest surprise was his recognition that the Church ***was*** *in crisis, and his view that the crisis focused on the family, leading him to call an Extraordinary Synod on the Family.*

The evidence of that crisis – both qualitative and quantitative – had been accumulating for decades, but the leaders of the institutional Church had not taken the trouble to study it. At world level the Catholic nuptiality rate had fallen from 11.8 per thousand Catholic population in 1971 to 4.4 in 2011. Over the decades since Humanae Vitae total nuptiality rates fell, in country after country, as marriage as an institution declined in popularity. But they fell much more steeply in the Catholic community. This is particularly revealing in countries where the majority of the population are Catholic. So that in Mexico, for example, the ***total*** *nuptiality rate fell 24% over the years 1971-2008, but the* ***Catholic*** *nuptiality rate fell 45%. Catholics were still getting married, but large numbers of them preferred to get married without the rites of the Church, or were refused a marriage with Catholic rites. The Church's own statistics since 1968 reveal a massive rejection of Catholic marriage by Catholics, or the rejection of the faithful by the institutional Church..*

Analysis of Catholic baptismal statistics also provides compelling evidence of crisis. At world level Catholic child baptismal rates fell 52% over the period 1971 to 2011. In South America the rate fell 61%. The faithful had protested at Humanae Vitae in 1968, and they have continued to do so ever since, refusing to be bound by the official teaching of the Church. Again, there are interesting comparisons in mainly Catholic countries between the ***Catholic*** *child baptismal rate and the* ***total*** *crude birth rate.*

Although the Roman Curia does not collect statistics of Sunday Mass attendance, the figures collected by Episcopal Conferences in some European countries show that by 2012 the Mass attendance rate (per thousand Catholic population) had fallen to 118 in Austria, 209 in England & Wales, 118 in Germany, and 254 in Scotland, and (in 2011) to 53 in the Netherlands.

One disaster widely predicted in the later 1950s and early 1960s did not materialise - the expected crisis of world overpopulation. Demographers failed to anticipate both the extent and the effects of technological and scientific innovation, rising standards of living, better personal and public health, better education, improvements in governance and reductions in corruption.

There were improvements in the expectation of life at birth, for both males and females, between 1950-5 and 2005-10. These were particularly marked in the Third World and in developed countries that had been devastated during World War II.

As parents became aware of the falls in infant, child and adolescent death rates they came to appreciate that it was no longer necessary to have the same large families as their own parents and grandparents. With rising living standards they also became aware of the increasing costs of a large family. They reacted very rationally by having fewer children and giving them better care and attention.

As a result of this fundamental change in population dynamics the latest most likely projection of world population suggests that it will stabilise at about nine billion from about 2100. The official teaching of the Church on contraception has had little or no effect on world population, because the laity have increasingly ignored what Popes and bishops have told them about its wickedness. The main damage has been done by governments in China and India whose population control measures have disturbed the gender balance, with very damaging social consequences.

PART I. THE DEVELOPMENT OF THE CRISIS

The beginning of the crisis

In 1968 the encyclical *Humanae Vitae* engulfed the Church in crisis. In 1930 the encyclical of Pope Pius XI, *Casti Connubii*, had created immense difficulties for the laity, many of whom had been using rather unreliable methods of birth control, generically described by moralists as Onanism. The encyclical required confessors to be proactive in ensuring that penitents understood that all forms of contraception were gravely sinful. Pamphlets on its evils were found in profusion in churches. The marriages of many Catholics who complied were wrecked. The religious practice of many was abandoned, while some just quit the Church altogether.

Then in 1950 and 1952 three addresses of Pope Pius XII relaxed the ban on contraception by allowing the use of the Ogino-Knaus method of confining sexual intercourse to the 'safe' or infertile period, for medical, eugenic, economic and social motives. This was well-publicised in the West, and supported by official Church agencies that encouraged research and development for a decade or more.

The Suenens initiatives

However, by the late 1950s and early 1960s obedient Catholic couples who were using one or more of these methods to regulate their families were finding that they were damaging their marital life. Confessors were increasingly aware of this, and so were some bishops, like Archbishop Suenens in Belgium. Since 1958 he had arranged annual gatherings of experts – priests, doctors and social scientists – at Louvain to discuss these issues. Following discussions with others in London in July, 1962, these gatherings morphed in 1963 into a formal organisation, SELIPO, the *Secretariat de Liaison pour les Etudes de Population,* hosted by the University of Louvain.

The first meeting of SELIPO, organised by Pere Henri de Riedmatten OP, representative of the Holy See in Geneva, lasted three days, 23-25 May, 1963. About a dozen attended: theologians, doctors, economists, demographers and sociologists. De Riedmatten explained that the Holy See was very aware of the pressure on national governments trying to persuade the United Nations to take a more proactive role in encouraging and supporting birth control programmes throughout the world. It needed expert advice on how to deal with this, and that was why SELIPO had been set up.

The Pontifical Commission

In March, 1963, Pope John XXIII had accepted Suenens' recommendation to establish the Pontifical Commission on Population, Family & Birth, with the same remit[1]. Six experts, half of those who attended the SELIPO meeting in May, were appointed to serve on the Commission. They had their first meeting, at Louvain, on 12-13 October, 1963. De Riedmatten's twenty-two page report on the meeting was 'quite orthodox and lacked even a hint of disagreement or dissent' (McClory, 1955: 42-3).

The Commission met in Rome in April, 1964. By that time Robert Blair's work[2] as correspondent in Europe for *Time* magazine had uncovered widespread evidence that the clergy and bishops in the Netherlands, Belgium, France and Germany were well aware of the dissatisfaction with 'rhythm' methods, and the popular enthusiasm for 'the pill'. Pope Paul VI doubled the size of the Commission, appointing five theologians, all priests – including Bernard Haering – and two lay sociologists. The Commission

[1] It later became clear that the SELIPO meetings had two functions. One was to assess the suitability of those who attended to serve on the Commission, as it was later enlarged. The late Dr John Marshall was 'quietly taken aside by de Riedmatten at the [SELIPO] 1963 conference' and told that the Pope 'had set up a small commission to look at specific questions with relation to population and would like him to serve on it (McClory, 1995: 41). The other was to allow a free and confidential exchange of views and information between Commission members and other experts. Apart from an intermission of one year the SELIPO meetings continued up to 1970, and possibly beyond.

[2] Described in his book *The Encyclical that never was* (1987), also published as *The Politics of Sex and religion (1985).*

met again, only two months later, for an emergency session – prompted by the then very public awareness of the concerns of Catholic couples. Another two priests had been appointed, one of them a theologian.

Until the June meeting, McClory (1965: 53) remarked:

> The members had seen themselves as court advisers to the Holy See, operating more or less strictly within the limits of the relevant Encyclicals and traditional theology. Haering had suggested moving beyond that, but their recommendations from the first two sessions indicated that caution prevailed.

De Riedmatten told them that there was to be a public pronouncement on 23 June, and that the Pope wanted answers on three questions:

> What is the relationship of primary and secondary ends of marriage? What are the major responsibilities of married couples? How do rhythm and the pill relate to responsible parenthood?

The Commission could not answer these questions before the session ended, and on 23 June, in a speech to the College of Cardinals at the Vatican, Paul VI revealed the existence of the Commission.

For Catholic couples his statement indicated that there was doubt about the official position of the Church over birth control. The Pope added that for the time being the rules laid down by Pius XII must be considered valid.

But theologically literate Catholics in the West were aware that *in dubium libertas,* and huge numbers took advantage of that *libertas*[3].

The Commission did not conclude its work until 24 June, 1966, two years later. By that time the lay experts, and the married couples representing the concerns and views of wives and husbands, had been phased out, leaving the theologians to draft their conclusions, and to discuss them with the sixteen cardinals and bishops who were to approve the report and submit it to the Pope.

McClory (1995: 127) wrote that the fifteen cardinals and bishops present voted first on three propositiona and then on giving formal assent to the report. Only one voice was heard in opposition, that of Colombo, the Pope's theologian:

> His Holiness will never accept the proposition that contraception is not intrinsically evil .... He would agree only to this: a letter to the world's bishops telling them their people are not to be disturbed. It is not necessary to disturb couples who practise contraception; close your eyes.

---

[3] I cannot recall anyone dissenting from the Church's official teaching, or even expressing doubts, at the 1963 and 1964 meetings of SELIPO. At the 1965 meeting, not realising that he was a member of the Commission, I asked John Marshall privately what his personal view was of the morality of contraception. He replied succinctly: *in dubium libertas.*

The vote on the formal assent is not known, or indeed whether there was a formal vote.

The next day the short pastoral document that Bishop Dupuy had prepared as an introduction to the report was read, discussed and approved. It read in part:

> All this teaching … has in many countries contributed powerfully to a deeper understanding of marriage and the demands of marriage union …. What is condemned is not the regulation of conception but a selfish married life, refusing creative opening out of the family circle …. As for the means that husband and wife can legitimately employ, it is their task to decide this together, without drifting into arbitrary decisions, but always taking into account the objective criteria of morality (McClory, 1995: 127-8).

On 28 June, 1966, Cardinal Doepfner and de Riedmatten presented the report and the Pastoral Introduction to Paul VI, along with the three-foot stack of twelve bound volumes of background material. Doepfner wrote to Bishop Reuss: 'I got the impression that the Holy Father is very uncertain and hesitant in the whole question' (McClory, 1995: 126).

Ottaviani and the Holy Office

McClory (1995: 129-30) commented that

> That some observers wondered why Cardinal Ottaviani, the Commission's president at the final Session, did not make the formal presentation of the material himself. The reason appears to be that Ottaviani, Father Ford, and others were already hard at work at the office of the Congregation of the Faith, preparing an unauthorised alternative report. On July 1, three days after Doepfner's audience, Ottaviani met with Pope Paul and presented him with a document repudiating what the majority had decided. It was basically Ford's so-called Minority Report, written the previous May as a working paper for the Commission and endorsed only by Ford and three other theologians. This marked the beginning of a long process that would culminate with *Humanae Vitae*

There are many detailed accounts of what happened between the delivery of the Commission's report and the publication of *Humanae Vitae* in August, 1968. The most important development was the publication of what was mis-described as the Majority Report, and two working papers, leaked to Mgr Alting von Geusau and passed on by him to the *National Catholic Reporter*, which published them on 15 April, 1967, and copied them to *The Tablet* in London.

Catholic couples in the West, still worried that Pius XII's ruling on rhythm methods was the Church's last word on contraception, now felt morally free to use the Pill and other methods like the coil.

Publication of *Humanae Vitae*

Well-informed Catholics around the world knew what the Pope's Commission had reported, and were outraged by his rejection of its recommendations. The protests in some countries lasted well over a year. In terms of the doctrine of 'reception'[4] the encyclical was more than not 'received': it was manifestly rejected, although many of those who rejected it so emphatically in 1968 had been respecting *Casti Connubii* decades earlier.

The uproar was not confined to the laity. Large numbers of secular and regular clergy protested publicly, while many more let it be known to friends that they did not accept *Humanae Vitae.* Despite the efforts of laity, dismayed at the prospect of losing large numbers of priests who were highly committed to Vatican II and its implementation, there was a steady trickle who abandoned their priestly vocation and 're-joined' the laity. They were still committed to the Church as the People of God, and to the mission that Christ gave his Church, but they were not prepared to serve institutional leaders who had betrayed the trust of their people, and defended the indefensible, in order to maintain their authority.

Although very few lay men and women studied for degrees in theology in the 1960s[5] one had completed two very thorough studies of the changes over the centuries in the official teaching of the Church, Dr John Noonan, professor of law at Notre Dame, Director of the Natural Law Institute and editor of *Natural Law Forum.* In 1957 he had published *The Scholastic Analysis of Usury.* He was invited to act as consultant to the Pontifical Commission, and in 1965, while it was still deliberating, he published *Contraception. A History of its Treatment by the Catholic Theologians and Canonists.* The view that 'the Church' had always proclaimed doctrines that it had received from Christ was subjected to critical examination as journalists discovered more of the detail of what had been said and done while the Commission was sitting, and subsequently.

While large numbers of priests abandoned their vocations, bishops and episcopal conferences in general seemed to acquiesce and saw no reason ro request an extraordinary synod to discuss the encyclical. It seemed

---

[4] See Yves M.Congar, 'Reception as an Ecclesiastical Reality', *Concilium* 77 (1972), 57-76, and Avery Dulles 'The Question of Non-Reception', *America,* November, 1986.

[5] In France Prof. Gabriel Le Bras was a historian of the canon law who turned his attention to religious sociology after the War.

that most of the bishops who had left Rome in 1965 had already forgotten what they had declared during Vatican II about collegiality[6]. During the four and a half decades since 1968 the timidity of bishops round the world suggests that most of them – especially those appointed since 1978 – have forgotten that Paul successfully challenged Peter.

Towards the end of the century there was another spate of books about the Commission, and about *Humanae Vitae* and its aftermath, as more of the by then elderly participants wrote or gave accounts to journalists. And others tried to assess the consequences of what happened, and did not happen, in the 1960s

In these accounts what was particularly revealing were the unguarded remarks made by some of the participants in the discussions of the Commission. They revealed two different concerns of the theologians and bishops who insisted that *Casti Connubii* was irreformable. Neither concern was about getting to the truth. The first was about the effect of any changes in the teaching of *Casti Connubii*, and the modifications made by Pope Pius XII, on perceptions of the authority of the Magisterium. The second was about the speakers' concern about themselves, which can only be described as narcissistic. This is discussed in Chapter Six.

PART II. THE AFTERMATH OF HUMANAE VITAE

Some statistical data

It is difficult to disentangle the effects of *Humanae Vitae* from those of Vatican II, and the leadership of three Popes – Paul VI, John Paul II and Benedict – and more recently the impact of the scandals over priestly paedophilia, and its treatment by bishops and the Roman Curia. But using the statistics published in the *Statistical Yearbook of the Church*, the sources of Table 1A and Table 1B, it is possible to get some idea of what happened to the readiness of Catholics to use the rites of the Church for their marriages, and their readiness to conceive and give birth to children, and to have them baptised.

At continental and sub-continental levels it is difficult to compare the data in the *Statistical Yearbook of the Church* with that published in the United Nations *Demographic Yearbook* as their territorial arrangement is very different. Instead, both Catholic nuptiality and national nuptiality rates are set out in Table 2 so that they can be compared. This table is for states whose population in 1950 exceeded 20 million. However, those for which

---

[6] Decades later, Philip Kaufman (1995: 90-102) gave a detailed account of the reactions of episcopal conferences to *Humanae Vitae* in his book *Why You Can Disagree and Remain a Faithful Catholic* (New York:Crossroads).

important data is not available have been excluded. So too has Iran, where the Catholic population is miniscule.

The nuptiality rates in Table 1A show that the willingness – or ability - of Catholics across the world to use the rites of the Church for marriage has fallen from 11.8 per thousand in 1971, three years after *Humanae Vitae*, to 4.4 in 2011. This fall is seen in every continent, though it is particularly marked in Europe and Oceania (effectively Australia and New Zealand). Within continents (as defined by the Central Statistics Office of the Church) it has been particularly acute in North America and South America. It was least marked in continental Central America and Asia.

Table 1A. Nuptiality rates[7] per 1,000 Catholic population, 1971-2011

Territory	**1971**	**1991**	**2001**	**2006**	**2011**
Africa	**8.3**	**4.9**	**4.5**	**4.1**	**3.4**
North America	14.9	9.3	6.2	4.7	3.7
Cont. Cent. America	9.9	8.6	8.2	6.3	6.3
Antilles Central America	5.0	2.3	2.8	1.7	1.3
South America	9.7	7.0	1.6	3.8	3.2
America	**10.5**	**8.8**	**5.2**	**4.4**	**5.2**
Asia: Middle East	8.0	6.1	7.5	7.8	6.1
Asia: remainder	11.8	10.6	11.0	9.7	8.6
Asia	**11.6**	**10.4**	**10.9**	**9.7**	**8.5**
Europe	**13.8**	**8.4**	**6.6**	**5.2**	**4.5**
Oceania	**13.8**	**7.4**	**4.6**	**4.1**	**3.6**
WORLD	**11.8**	**7.8**	**6.1**	**5.2**	**4.4**

The disenchantment with marriage seen in Table 1A is not confined to the Catholic population. Whether it has been more marked or less for Catholics will be considered later. It demonstrates how damaging *Humanae Vitae* was to the understanding of marriage that was solemnly stated at Trent. Catholics theologically literate have embraced the principle that at marriage the bride and groom confer the sacrament of marriage on each other, andhave simply gone elsewhere for the formal recognition and recording of their marriage. The effective power of the Papacy and the Episcopal College to command compliance of the People of God has been shredded by its abuse and misuse.

[7] For total populations the nuptiality rate is twice the marriage rate. But Catholics sometimes marry non-Catholics. So for them the nuptiality rate is the number of Catholics married with the rites of the Church per thousand Catholic population.

Table 1B. Baptismal rates per 1,000 Catholic population, 1971-2011

Territory	Child baptismal rates				
	1971	**1991**	**2001**	**2006**	**2011**
Africa	**32.0**	**20.5**	**16.4**	**14.4**	**13.0**
North America	21.5	17.8	14.6	12.4	10.8
Cont. Cent. America	36.5	23.4	19.0	17.4	16.7
Antilles Central America	25.1	14.2	11.5	9.8	9.4
South America	26.9	18.5	13.3	12.1	10.5
America	**27.8**	**19.3**	**14.8**	**13.3**	**11.9**
Asia: Middle East	16.7	8.2	7.5	6.6	5.7
Asia: remainder	34.1	24.4	21.0	19.5	18.6
Asia	**33.5**	**23,8**	**20.7**	**19.2**	**16.9**
Europe	**16.7**	**10.5**	**8.5**	**8.0**	**7.5**
Oceania	**27.0**	**17.5**	**13.2**	**12.3**	**11.4**
WORLD	**24.1**	**17.2**	**13.9**	**12.7**	**11.6**

Table 2A. Catholic Nuptiality rates, per thousand Catholic population, in the most populous states, 1971-2008

State	1971	1991	2001	2006	2007	2008
N. America						
Canada	16.9	6.9	4.2	3.1	2.8	2.7
Mexico	11.4	9.2	8.0	6.6	6.3	6.3
USA	12.4	9.8	6.6	5.1	4.9	4.7
S. America						
Argentine	12.1	8.8	4.0	3.9	3.6	3.6
Peru	8.8	6.4	3.7	3.4	3.2	3.5
Venezuela	5.9	3.0	2.4	1.8	2.5	2.7
Asia						
Japan	17.1	10.8	6.2	4.1	4.0	3.8
Korea, South	13.9	12.4	9.0	8.4	8.1	7.5
Europe						
France	13.4	5.9	4.8	3.6	3.4	3.5
Germany (All)	9.5	6.4	3.4	3.1	3.1	3.1
Hungary	12.5	7.2	2.5	3.5	3.5	3.3
Italy	15.4	9.8	8.0	6.5	6.7	6.0
Netherlands	16.9	6.4	4.0	2.5	2.5	2.3
Poland	15.5	12.3	8.6	9.2	9.7	10.1
Romania	9.5	3.7	5.3	5.3	6.3	5.6
Spain	14.4	8.9	8.2	5.6	5.4	5.2

Table 1B gives some idea of what has happened to the birth rates of the Catholic community since *Humanae Vitae*. The Catholic baptismal figures include all baptisms up to the age of seven, as well as those of older people. But by treating these baptismal statistics as equivalent to live births they can be used to calculate the crude birth rate of the Catholic population[8].

Table 1B shows that for the world as a whole the Catholic child baptismal rates fell from 24.1 in 1971 to 11.6 in 2011, a fall of 51.9% over forty years. This fall occurred in all the continents etc. for which figures are given in the *Statistical Yearbook of the Church.* Table 3A shows how these falls in the reproductive rates of the Catholic population occurred in the

Table 2B. Total Nuptiality rates, in the most populous states, 1971-2008

State	Total nuptiality rates (i.e. 2 x marriage rate)					
	1971	**1995**	**2001**	**2006**	**2007**	**2008**
N. America						
Canada	17.8	11.0	9.4	9.2	9.2	9.0
Mexico	14.4	14.6	13.0	11.2	11.2	11.0
USA	21.2	17.8	16.4	14.8	14.6	14.2
S. America						
Argentine	...	9.2	7.0	7.0	7.0	...
Peru	7.0	...	...	6.4	6.6	6.4
Venezuela	12.4	7.6	6.6	6.6	6.8	...
Asia						
Japan	20.8	12.6	12.6	11.6	11.4	11.6
Korea, South	...	17.6	13.6	13.6	14.0	13.6
Europe						
France	15.8	8.8	9.8	8.6	8.6	8.6
Germany (All)	14.2	10.6	9.4	9.0	9.0	9.2
Hungary	18.2	10.4	8.6	8.8	8.2	8.0
Italy	15.0	10.2	9.6	8.4	8.4	8.4
Netherlands	18.6	10.6	10.0	8.8	8.8	9.2
Poland	17.8	10.8	10.0	11.8	13.0	...
Romania	14.2	13.6	11.8	13.6	17.6	13.8
Spain	14.8	10.2	10.2	9.4	9.2	8.4

most populous states for which figures are available. However, the conclusion that emerges most clearly from both Table 1B and Table 3A is that, despite all the Papal condemnations of the use of contraception by Catholics, in the 1960s and later, the Catholic community has been using it on an increasing scale. The halving of the child baptismal rate could not

[8] However, they distort the figures for two reasons. First, they **exclude** the births of those babies and young children who were born alive but not then baptised until they were over seven. Second, they **include** (in the wrong year) the births of those born between the ages of one and seven, as well as those of unbaptised converts.

have occurred if Catholic couples throughout most parts of the world had not only continued using forbidden methods but had increased their use year by year since 1971. The storm of protest in 1968 was one expression of the rejection of *Humanae Vitae* by the People of God. But the steady increase in the use of contraception over forty years was a far more practical expression of that rejection.

However, the massive rejection of *Humanae Vitae* over four decades is evidence of something much more fundamental. The clear motive of those who were determined that Pope Paul VI should reject the Commission's report was to sustain the authority of the Papacy by insisting

Table 3A. Catholic baptismal rates in most populous states, 1971-2008

State	**1971**	**1995**	**2001**	**2006**	**2007**	**2008**
N. America						
Canada	19.3	13.1	9.4	7.9	7.6	7.6
Mexico	37.8	20.1	19.8	18.7	17.9	18.7
USA	22.1	17.6	15.7	13.4	13.6	13.5
S. America						
Argentina	21.7	17.1	15.2	14.0	13.8	13.9
Peru	25.2	12.3	11.0	9.5	9.8	9.8
Venezuela	29.3	16.2	15.7	15.7	15.0	15.3
Asia						
India	29.1	17.1	17.2	16.2	16.3	16.1
Japan	17.9	11.3	8.9	6.6	6.5	6.6
Korea, South	28.4	11.7	7.6	9.6	5.0	4.8
Philippines	35.6	27.2	23.9	21.6	20.7	19.8
Europe						
France	14.7	8.5	8.0	7.0	6.9	6.7
Germany (All)	8.7	8.7	7.6	6.9	6.9	7.0
Hungary	24.1	7.7	7.4	8.7	8.7	8.6
Italy	16.8	8.6	8.1	7.8	7.6	7.6
Netherlands	18.3	7.1	8.2	6.7	6.1	6.2
Poland	16.4	11.8	9.8	9.5	9.9	10.5
Romania	...	4.4	5.9	5.8	5.9	6.0
Spain	20.0	8.5	8.2	7.5	7.6	7.6

that a doctrine, once it had been proclaimed publicly by the Pope, could not be reformed. In this too, the Roman Curia failed totally. Increasingly, those previously ready to heed statements of the Pope – or made by the Roman Curia on his behalf – became unwilling to do so. If the Papacy could commit such an egregious misuse of the teaching authority of the Church over the morality of birth regulation, the People of God could have little confidence in any other moral or doctrinal statement issued. As the numbers of lay graduate theologians and professors of theology increased, official moral and doctrinal statements were increasingly treated as interesting, and to be considered seriously by theologians – but no more.

Despite its incomplete character, Table 3B allows us to make interesting comparisons between child baptismal rates and crude birth rates in some large countries. In Canada the baptismal rate in 2006 was 40.9% of the rate in 1971, but the crude birth rate was 64.9% of that in 1971. Not only was the Catholic baptismal rate in 2006 much lower than the crude birth rate in 2006 than in 1971, it had fallen much faster. The same changes

Table 3B. Crude birth rates in the most populous states, 1971-2008

State	1971	1995	2001	2006	2007	2008
N. America						
Canada	16.8	12.9	10.8	10.9	11.2	...
Mexico	...	24.6	...	...	...	...
USA	17.2	14.8	14.1	14.3	14.3	...
S. America						
Argentina	...	18.9	18.2	17.9	17.8	...
Peru	35.2	26.2	23.9	...	...	...
Venezuela	39.2	23.8	21.4	23.9	22.4	...
Asia						
India	...	25.4	...	23.5	23.1	22.8
Japan	19.3	9.5	9.2	8.7	8.6	8.7
Korea, South	...	15.8	11.8	9.2	10.0	9.4
Philippines	25.4	28.6	...	19.1	19.7	...
Europe						
France	17.2	12.5	13.0	12.9	12.7	12.7
Germany (All)	12.7	9.4	8.9	8.2	8.3	8.3
Hungary	14.5	11.0	9.5	9.9	9.7	9.7
Italy	16.8	9.2	9.2	9.5	9.5	9.5
Netherlands	17.2	12.3	12.6	11.3	11.1	11.1
Poland	17.1	11.2	9.5	9.8	10.2	10.2
Romania	19.6	10.4	10.0	10.2	10.0	10.0
Spain	19.6	9.3	10.1	11.0	11.0	11.0

can be seen in the data for the USA. The baptismal rate was lower than the crude birth rate in 2006, and in that year was only 60.6% of that in 1971. Yet the crude birth rate in 2006, at 14.3, was higher than the Catholic baptismal rate, and the former was 83.1% of the crude birth rate in 1971.

In Venezuela the Catholic baptismal rate in 2006, at 15.7 per thousand, was well below the crude birth rate of 23.9. The latter was 61.0% of that in 1971, while the baptismal rate was only 53.6% of the 1971 rate. In Japan the baptismal rate in 2008, at 6.6, was well below the crude birth rate of 8.7. The Catholic rate in 2008 was only 33.9% of the rate in 1971, while the crude birth rate in 2008 was 45.1% of the 1971 rate. In the Philippines the baptismal rate in 2006, at 21.6, was above the crude birth rate, 19.1. But the latter was 75.2% of the 1971 figure, while the Catholic rate was only 60.7% of the 1971 rate.

In France the baptismal rate in 2008, at 6.7, was little over half of the crude birth rate, 12.7. The Catholic rate was only 45.6% of 1971, while the crude birth rate was 73.8% of that in 1971. In Germany as a whole the baptismal rate in 2008, at 7.0, was below the crude birth rate of 8.3, and had fallen to 80.5% of 1971, while the crude birth rate in 2008 was 65.4% of 1971. In Hungary the baptismal rate in 2008, at 8.6, was below that crude birth rate, 9.7. In 2008 it was only 35.7% of the 1971 rate, while the crude birth rate was 66.9% of 1971. In Italy the baptismal rate in 2008, at 7.6, was below the crude birth rate, 9.5. The baptismal rate in 2008 was 45.2% of 1971, while the crude birth rate was 56.5 of 1971. In the Netherlands the baptismal rate in 2008, at 6.2, was little more than half the crude birth rate of 11.1. The baptismal rate in 2008 was only 33.9% that of 1971, while the crude birth rate was 64.5%. In Poland the baptismal rate in 2008 was a little lower than the crude birth rate, the latter being 59.6 % of the 1971 rate. The baptismal rate in 2008 was 64.0% of the 1971 rate. In Spain the baptismal rate in 2008, at 7.6 was just two-thirds of the crude birth rate, 11.0. It was only 38% of the baptismal rate in 1971, while the crude birth rate was 56.1%.

In summary, with slight qualifications in the cases of Germany and Poland, the baptismal rates had fallen much faster than the crude birth rates, and in country after country the latest birth rate was above the corresponding baptismal rate. The laity had not only fled from Catholic marriage, but had been so alienated from the institutional church that they had defied the leadership of the Church to the extent of declining to baptise many of the children they begot and conceived[9].

Table 4 provides evidence of the extent of alienation demonstrated by the Mass attendance rates of a number of European countries. Given the stress placed by the institutional church on Mass attendance and reception

---

[9] As late as February, 2014, one of the leading English bishops wrote to me, in response to a PRC report criticising the Church's official statistics system, that the members of his Department of the Catholic Bishops Conference considered that 'the actual figures were of little use without further analysis …. If people are leaving the church (or entering) then we really need to know the reasons, not just the numbers'. It seems that Francis Bergoglio, without being a statistician, had a very acute understanding of the reasons why Catholics were leaving the Church, recognised that they focused on marriage, sexuality and the family, and decided to summon an Extraordinary Synod to advise him on the issues. Unfortunately, the understanding of marriage, sexuality and the family among the men he summoned was limited to their experience of the family of orientation.

of the Eucharist, it is extraordinary that the General Statistical Questionnaire, sent annually by each diocese to the Roman Curia, does not ask for statistics on Mass attendance. Table 4 therefore includes only Mass attendance rates (per thousand Catholic population) collected by some European Episcopal conferences, based on counted attendance.

Table 4. Mass attendance rates of some European countries, 1958-2012 (Counted attendance at Sunday Mass, per 1,000 Catholic population).

Year	Austria	E & W	Germany	Netherlands	Scotland
1958	...	538		...	...
1960	...	533		...	...
1965	...	522		...	...
1967	...	491		...	521
1971	...	464		362	...
1980	...	386		222	...
1991	...	305		...	...
1995	...	...		...	343
1996	...	...		...	336
2001	...	236		84	311
2006	132	227		66	290
2011	120	208		53	252
2012	118	209	118	...	254

The statistical evidence set out in the tables above suggests three major conclusions. First, the Church has been in manifest or latent crisis ever since the publication of *Humanae Vitae*. Second, the faithful have increasingly ignored the views of three successive Popes, the Roman Curia, and the Episcopal College asserting the wickedness of contraception. Third, the teaching authority of the institutional church has been gravely damaged.

PART III. THE CRISIS THAT DID NOT HAPPEN

Why have birth rates declined?

From the discussions at the annual meetings of SELIPO, I know that the demographers appointed to serve on the Pontifical Commission shared the widely held view of experts at that time that the world could not sustain the current rate of population increase. With the much greater volume of statistical evidence that has become available in the last half century we can see that their fears were unfounded, and appreciate the weakness in their understanding of population growth. Table 5 sets out, for males and females, the expectation of life at birth between 1950-5 and 2005-10.

Over five decades the expectation of life at birth increased in every country except South Africa, for both males and females. For the countries listed in Table 2B the mean annual rates of increase in life expectancy at birth are set out in Table 6, separately for males and females.

Table 5. Expectation of life at birth, largest states, 1950-5 to 2005-10

Country	**1950-5**		**1970-5**		**2005-10**	
N. America	**M**	**F**	**M**	**F**	**M**	**F**
Canada	66.3	70.8	63.9	82.2	78.2	82.8
Mexico	48.1	51.1	59.4	63.4	73.7	78.6
USA	65.6	71.1	67.1	74.8	75.4	80.5
S. America						
Brazil	51.0	57.4	58.5	64.4	68.7	75.9
Colombia	44.1	45.9	58.5	61.2	69.2	76.7
Peru	42.4	44.4	53.3	55.9	70.6	75.9
Venezuela	52.2	56.3	62.9	66.6	70.8	76.8
Asia						
Japan	56.2	59.6	69.3	74.7	79.3	86.1
Philippines	44.6	47.5	56.9	60.0	64.5	71.3
Europe						
France	63.6	69.3	68.5	76.1	77.5	84.3
German FR	64.6	68.5	67.4	73.8	77.2	82.4
Hungary	63.5	67.3	66.9	72.6	69.5	77.6
Italy	63.7	67.2	69.0	74.9	78.6	84.4
Netherlands	70.6	72.9	71.2	77.2	78.1	82.2
Poland	58.6	64.2	66.8	73.8	71.2	79.9
Romania	...	...	66.3	70.8	69.6	76.8
Spain	59.8	64.3	69.7	75.0	77.2	83.8
UK	66.4	71.5	68.9	75.1	77.4	81.7

Sources: UN *Demographic Year Book* and UN *Statistical Yearbook*

There is a fairly clear divide between the developed countries (not devastated by war) on the one hand, and the developing countries (and those devastated by war) on the other. The former experienced relatively low mean annual increases in life expectation at birth, while the latter experienced high annual increases as they began to enjoy better incomes and personal and environmental health that the developed countries had had at the outset. The fall in age-specific death rates led to rises in age-specific expectations of life, not only at birth but at later ages.

Implications of higher expectations of life for population growth

Demographers in the early 1960s did not appreciate that world population was moving towards a long term stable balance as a result of the falls in death rates brought about by better provision for both personal and environmental health. These were the result not only of advances in medicine but also of the rising GDP per capita of the developing countries, reductions in corruption and improvements in governance.

Table 6. Mean annual rates of increase in life expectancy

Country	Period	Male	% pa	Female	% pa
N. America	**(years)**	**%**		**%**	
Canada	55	17.9	0.3	16.9	0.3
Mexico	55	53.2	1.0	53.8	1.1
USA	55	14.9	0.3	13.2	9.2
S. America					
Argentina	45	13.3	0.3	14.8	0.3
Brazil	55	34.7	0.6	32.2	0.6
Colombia	55	56.9	1.0	67.1	1.2
Peru	55	66.5	1.2	70.9	1.3
Venezuela	55	35.6	0.6	36.4	0.7
Asia					
India	50	48.1	1.0	60.2	1.2
Japan	55	41.1	0.7	44.5	0.8
Korea, South	50	49.7	1.0	55.1	1.1
Philippines	55	44.6	0.8	50.1	1.0
Europe					
France	55	21.9	0.4	21.6	0.4
German FR	55	19.5	0.4	20.3	0.4
Hungary	55	9.4	0.2	15.3	0.3
Italy	55	23.4	0.4	25.0`	0.5
Netherlands	55	10.5	0.2	12.8	0.2
Poland	55	21.5	0.4	24.5	0.4
Romania	50	5.1	0.1	18.2	0.3
Spain	55	29.1	0.5	30.3	0.6
UK	55	16.6	0.3	14.3	0.2

Source: Table 5.

Demographers did not understand that better living standards and better health would result for many populations in an appreciation among parents that they did not need to have such large families, in order to maintain the family farm or enterprise, or to ensure that there were working adult children who could support their parents in old age. This appreciation came slowly, as couples noticed fewer funerals of babies and children in their communities. They gradually developed the confidence that was already there in the developed world, that they would not be distressed in their later life if they did not have as many children as their own parents.

At the same time as parents became increasingly sceptical about the **future** benefits of a large family they became increasingly aware of the rising **current** costs of food, clothing, housing, education and recreation of large families. So two perceptions of social and cultural change were encouraging parents to have smaller and smaller families as the decades passed.

This has not yet led to falls in population, as the process takes several generations to work through. When parents aim at only two or three children and use contraceptive measures to achieve that, then the two or three will survive into old age as a result of better health. But so will the parents' own generation, of whom more will have survived infancy and childhood, and will benefit from better health throughout their lives. So the parents' generation will not die off as quickly as demographers had expected in the early 1960s. Then the survivors of the grandparents' generation will likewise live longer than the actuaries had predicted. So the world population will go on rising until it stabilises towards the end of this century, as a result of parental decisions taken generations earlier that they did not need to have as many children as their own parents.

The spread of contraceptive practices throughout the world will have made this possible, and as Catholics have manifestly rejected *Casti Connubii* and *Humanae Vitae* they too will continue to regulate their families, and in so doing will help to ensure that the natural environment is not destroyed by the need to feed, clothe, house and educate future generations. Then Christians can turn their attention to the rich and powerful who have no concern about their neighbours throughout the world, and want ever more of the world's resources for themselves. This would require changes in culture that would root out corruption, demand better government, and a secular acceptance of what Christians see as the Second Great Commandment.

Future world population growth

Population did go on rising after the 1960s, and it is still rising, but it is now accepted as most likely that it will stabilise at about nine billion from about 2100. And the social mechanism that will effect this, described above, is now widely accepted.

There have been famines, but on nothing like the scale of earlier periods. There have been wars, civil wars and natural disasters, corruption and bad government on a wide scale. But despite much hand-wringing and breast-beating by political and religious leaders, in almost every state in Table 5, expectations of life for both males and females at birth are in the period 2005-10 far better than in 1950-55. This could not have happened if the population had not been better fed, clothed, housed, cared far medically, and educated.

Without heeding the demands of politicians and Catholic bishops the people of the world have regulated their own reproduction very effectively as death rates have fallen. As a result, the latest medium projection of world population is for stabilisation at a little below nine billion after 2100. Brutal methods have been used by governments in China and India, and threats of damnation by Catholic bishops. Catastrophe has not arrived, and for this we have to thank economic growth, the advance of science, developments in public and personal health, and better international, national and local government. But, above all, Christians may thank God for giving the human species a nature that is different from that of all other species, in three respects: we have a unique ability to think, a unique ability to learn from experience, and between birth and adulthood we need two decades of love, nurture, care, socialisation, education and training

A conclusion, for now

There is therefore every reason for Catholics to be full of hope. Up to the resignation of Benedict Ratzinger, the Papacy, the Roman Curia – and the Episcopal College that has timidly endorsed whatever the Vatican has demanded since the end of Vatican II – have not succeeded in convincing the laity (or most of the priesthood) that contraception is morally wrong. In their efforts to do so they have created a huge divide between themselves and the People of God. The hundreds of millions of baptised Catholics who have been alienated since Vatican II seem to fall into four categories:

(a) Those who wanted nothing more to do with the Church, because they identified it with the institutional leadership, not the membership;
(b) Those divorced who wanted to re-marry with the rites of the Church, but were rejected;
(c) Those divorced who wanted to re-marry with the rites of the Church, but were unwilling to stigmatise their children as bastards;
(d) Those divorced who thought it would be a waste of time to seek an annulment.

There is no comprehensive statistical data that would allow us to estimate the numbers in each of these four categories.

Popes and prelates have done great damage to the Church of which they see themselves as leaders. Their statements on theological and moral issues are sometimes dismissed as not worth attention, sometimes debated seriously by the increasing numbers of lay theologians – and by the many priests who have suffered dreadfully at the hands of the CDF for offering alternative views – and occasionally heeded, as have many of the remarks of Francis Bergoglio.

In Chapter Six the theme of crisis will be picked up again to ask, first, how this crisis in the Church came about, so soon after an Ecumenical Council that was meant to provide an *aggiornamento*, a new readiness to face the reality of the world as it is, and not the world as it was in the sixteenth or nineteenth centuries. Second, what is it about the culture and structure of the institutional Church that caused it to fail so disastrously in the sixteenth century, the nineteenth, and in the five decades since the Bishops left Rome in 1965? Third, what measures could the Synods recommend that might protect the institutional Church from repeating the errors made since 1965 that have given rise to the current crisis, and avoid more damaging crises at a time of rapid social and cultural change.

Each of the following three chapters is devoted to developing a solution to one set of problems, first to pre-marital sexuality and co-habitation, then to sexuality and responsible parenthood in marriage, and finally to marital breakdown and the protection of the children. Then Chapter Five suggests a new approach to preparation for marriage, sexuality and the family - an approach that starts when the child, at age three or four, develops a memory, and ends in old age – and permanent long-term support for the family.

CHAPTER TWO
BETROTHAL, CO-HABITATION AND PROMISCUITY: PAST, PRESENT & FUTURE

SUMMARY

This chapter offers a solution to problems of pre-marital sexuality, co-habitation and promiscuity that have emerged on a massive scale since the Sixties, causing great damage to the social structures and cultures of the West. It reviews the history of Christian marriage up to the late Middle Ages, and focuses on the political factors that had by the end of the eleventh century shaped it, using Northern France as a case study. It demonstrates that this model of marriage dominated in the West - in the Latin Rite Catholic Church and the Churches of the Reformation - up until the mid-Twentieth Century. Since then it has been rejected on a massive scale.

The suggested solution to the problems of pre-marital sexuality, co-habitation and promiscuity is based on the practice of both secular societies and the Latin Rite Catholic Church during the first Christian millennium. The solution has three elements. The first is to accept now what the Christian Church accepted as late as the Council of Rome in 1069, that concubinage (pre-marital sexuality within co-habitation) and marriage are to some extent alternatives.

The second is to recognise betrothal - engagement, a public affirmation of the intention to marry - as a critically important stage in the process of getting married, and to restore it to its former dignity and importance. The third element is to recognise marriage as a process that begins with heterosexual friendship, is followed by courtship, and then recognised publicly at betrothal by both the secular community and the institutional Church as the first stage of marriage. From betrothal onward sexual intercourse would be expected and respected as morally legitimate, subject to one critical condition – that effective contraceptive measures are used to ensure that no child is conceived until the couple are formally married.

PART I. THE HISTORICAL BACKGROUND

In the Preface to his comprehensive study of the making of modern marriage in mediaeval France, *The Knight the Lady and the Priest,* Georges Duby (1983: xix-xx) wrote that his

> previous research had brought out the coexistence of two matrimonial moralities, one imposed by the priests and the other put into practice by the warriors who then formed the ruling class; also the conflict between these two models, which grew more acute

> during the eleventh century and then gradually died down, ending in the compromises that were to govern Western marriage practices for centuries.

He went on to explain that

> All educated people … would like to understand how the structures and rites at present disintegrating before our eyes came into being almost a thousand years ago, and thence why those rites and structures are falling apart today.

Thirty years later a newly elected Bishop of Rome at last recognised that they were indeed falling apart, and summoned an Extraordinary Synod on the Family. This chapter considers just one aspect of that falling apart – denied for forty-five years – and makes proposals that address it, the re-invention of betrothal and co-habitation as the first stage of marriage.

Duby (xx) went on to remark that in his study of mediaeval marriage he had been hearing about women all along, but the speakers were always men, 'representing members of the other sex as objects at once contemptible, terrifying and tempting'. Almost all were celibate, with no personal experience of marital sexuality and the family of procreation.

Duby's book is an excellent source on the double transition that started in the tenth century, as the migrations and conquests of the Celtic, Frankish, Germanic tribes, and the Vikings in the West, came to a gradual and brutal conclusion, marking the end of the so-called Dark Ages and the start of the feudal Middle Ages.

This was matched by the transition within the institutional Church in the West from its gravely weakened state at the end of the Dark Ages to the assertive rigorist Church determined to enforce its power over the various manifestations of the State – the Holy Roman Emperor, the kings and nobles – and demonstrate that in many important matters, like the enforcement of the criminal law, it would not 'render to Caesar the things which are Caesar's'. Rigorism over marriage became a useful too in its struggle to control Caesar.

The argument of this chapter is that one aspect of the disintegration of the structures and rites of marriage, finally detailed at Trent in the sixteenth century, can be repaired by the re-recognition of betrothal as the first stage of marriage.

Pre-Christian marriage

However, a study of betrothal has to start far earlier that the eighth century AD. In Jewish law (Torah), first exemplified by Abraham, marriage consisted of two separate acts, *erusin,* the betrothal ceremony, and *nissuin,* the actual marriage ceremony. These two ceremonies were later adopted in Greek culture as the *gamos* and *engeysis* rituals. Roman marriage law borrowed from Judaism the giving of the ring at engagement, after swearing the oath of marriage intent.

What almost all Indo-European cultures shared until the Renaissance were six features:

- Marriage was a matter for the (male) heads of households;
- It represented an agreement of the (male) head of the woman's family to hand her over to the son of the (male) head of the receiving family;
- It was focused on the reproduction of the tribe, clan or dynasty;
- It was regulated by the civil laws of the society, tribe or clan;
- It was a ritualised event; and
- It and its associated rituals had a religious character;

There were other features which varied:

- The extent of the involvement of the parties (who could be babies);
- The extent of the parties' ability to veto the transaction;
- The payment of a bride-price or dowry.

Schillebeeckx (1965: 3-18) gives an account of marriage in the Greek and Roman environments in the millennium before Christianity. First, it was a 'sacral' event. For both Greeks and Romans marriage was not originally based on interpersonal relationships, nor directly on the procreative act, but on the 'religion of the hearth'. The woman was transferred from the family religion of her father's household to that of the bridegroom's household. First, in her father's house she was handed over, in the *traditio puellae.* Then she was solemnly taken to the house of her bridegroom, in the *domum ductio.* At the threshold , Schillebeeckx (6) records that

> after a simulated abduction by force, she was carried by the bridegroom over the threshold of his, which she herself was not permitted to touch.

It was at this point that the religious ceremony of marriage took place, the incardination into the new household religion. After prayers and offerings the *confarreatio* took place, the sharing of the wedding cake, whereby

> The bride and groom entered into communion with each other through communion with the household gods.

Schillebeeckx (7-10) emphasises that it was the principle of the household religion which provided the basis for the monogamous and essentially indissoluble character of marriage. Children were needed to perpetuate the family's religion, and the husband and father was the real priest of the household.

However, the secularisation that took place in Greek and Roman society from the seventh to the fifth centuries BC gradually dissociated marriage from its original foundations. The sacral *confarreatio* was no longer practised among the people.

> The new form of marriage was based on the inclinations of the intending partners and concluded by means of their mutual consent (Schillebeeckx: 10-12)

Morality was divorced from religion, and its rationale was sought in the Natural Law.

At the time of the Empire betrothal was arranged by the fathers of each family, the *stipulatio*, sometimes done when the children were still very young. Schillebeeckx notes (12-13) that this betrothal was a contract without any form of law, and expressed in the adoption in the West of the *arrha* in betrothals, a pledge which often took the form of an engagement ring.

The marriage itself was conducted without any form of law. The ancient *confarreatio* and its successors had disappeared. Marriages were concluded by mutual consent. Validity depended on the parties' *consensus,* on the *domum-ductio*, and on their subsequent living together – not on actual sexual intercourse.

This Roman law of marriage differed from later canon law in that it was purely secular, and the parties were bound only so long as they mutually agreed. It remained a strictly personal and family affair. During the Empire the *tabulae nuptiales* came into use, stating that the marriage was undertaken 'in order to bring forth children' (Schillebeeckx: 14-15).

Christian marriages in the early centuries

Christian marriage was much the same as that of pagans. The Synod of Elvira, c.306, accepted that the marriages of baptised Christians would be celebrated like those of unbaptised pagans. The Church accepted too the subjection of her members to the Roman legislature, and that matrimonial cases would be brought before the civil law courts (Schillebeeckx: 18-19). For Christians as for pagans marriage was a family affair, though later the decision to marry was more and more taken by the two partners. Schillebeeckx notes (20) that in the case of marriages between Christians clerical intervention was regarded as superfluous;

> … marriage was above all seen to be a secular reality which had to be experienced 'in the Lord'. The father of the house was responsible for the Christian way of life of everyone in the household, and thus also for their choice of a Christian partner in marriage.

The intervention of the clergy was required only in the case of marriages of the clergy and catechumens. Bishops were involved only in the cases of orphans, and women who had been unfaithful to vows of virginity (Schillebeeckx: 24-5).

Schillebeeckx (28-29) remarks that

> there is no suggestion in [Tertullian *Ad uxorem*] of a marriage contract before the forum of the church. '*Ecclesia conciliat*' means that the church 'founds' Christian marriage. It does not mean that marriage may be entered into only with ecclesiastical permission, or that the bishop or priest, as guardian, should take over the role of the father .... The whole of *Ad uxorem* is directed against the contracting of marriages with pagans..... The marriage of a Christian woman with a pagan provided the point of departure for this book.... A 'church marriage' according to this context is therefore a marriage between two baptised Christians; it is only such marriages which receive the blessing and consent of the heavenly Father. .. The phrase *Ecclesia conciliat* in fact confirms the civil and family basis of the Christian marriage contract, since ... the father's consent was necessary for a valid marriage.

Schillebeeckx concludes (31-3):

> Tertullian says nothing at all about an ecclesiastical liturgy of marriage, with a nuptial mass and a priestly solemnisation of marriage, but is referring to the Christian experience of marriage which is brought about by both partners' sharing the same faith, by their joint participation in the eucharist, by their practice of Christian charity, and by their praying together at home.... Tertullian's text seems to me to be of great dogmatic importance. It represents the intermediate stage between the still undifferentiated biblical assertions about marriage and the later assertion of the sacramental nature of marriage between baptised persons. At this stage, a 'church marriage' was still a valid contract of marriage made civilly and in the family between two baptised persons and relating to the secular sphere. There is no direct reference here to a separate ecclesiastical or liturgical solemnisation of marriage.

Christian marriage from fourth to eleventh centuries

The first evidence of a nuptial mass, with a priestly solemnisation of marriage contracted civilly and in the family, dates (Schillebeeckx: 32-3) from the fourth and fifth centuries, and relates to requirements that the lower orders of the clergy were bound to have their marriages solemnised by a priest. As late as 866 Pope Nicholas I, in his *Responsum ad Bulgaros,* confirmed the validity of marriages by mutual consent, even if all family, civil and ecclesiastical ceremonies were lacking.

During the Dark Ages the institutional Church had to cope with the marital laws and customs, and moral understandings, of waves of invaders and migrants.

Germanic

In Germanic law marriage was seen as a contract between two tribes or extended family groups, rather than as a contract between the bride and bridegroom themselves (Schillebeeckx: 33-7). In the pre-Frankish period this took the form of a single legal proceeding, but later it was separated into two: the betrothal and the marriage itself. Later still Germanic law began to emphasise the mutual consent of the two partners.

Schillebeeckx (35) noted that it is not clear

> whether the mutual consent to the marriage was sufficient in itself, if it was not given a concrete form in the giving of the ring and the wedding presents. The handing over of the bride by her father or guardian was the most important condition.... Each different tribe had its own marriage customs, and these were strictly observed with the aim of preventing any later doubts and disputes over the validity of the marriage.

By the eleventh century, Schillebeeckx (36-7) notes, the proceedings were taking place in three stages: the first was the proposal and the betrothal, followed by the mutual consent to marry, and finally the wedding feast, which began with the bringing of the bride to her new home, the festive meal, the solemn entry into the bridal chamber and the consummation of the marriage. This third stage gradually came to be regarded as conclusive evidence of the marriage contract.

Frankish

Again there were two stages, the betrothal and the marriage itself. Schillebeeckx noted (37-38) that the betrothal of a girl was decided by her father and the tribe. The betrothal was effected by the payment of a fixed sum of money. The taking of the bride to the bridegroom's house was subject to statutory regulation, and the public character of marriage was stressed in the Roman Merovingian law of the Franks. At the conclusion of the marriage itself the bridegroom acknowledged in the presence of witnesses his responsibility to protect and represent his wife.

Western Gothic

Originally Arians, these were not converted in Spain until the sixth century (Schillebeeckx: 38), and it was through them that betrothal by means of the *arrha* (the engagement ring) penetrated to Rome and the whole of the West:

> For the Western Goths betrothal and marriage were above all tribal affairs, as they were for all the Germanic tribes ....The most important proof of a validly contracted marriage was the giving of the dowry.... These customs were also observed by Christians.

Celtic and Anglo-Saxon

Schillebeeckx (38-9) notes that both the Celts and the Anglo-Saxons

> originally regarded the women simply as merchandise, and marriage consequently above all as a sort of deed of purchase or conveyance. The price was paid to the 'guardian' (or to the tribe) of the bride. It was not until the eleventh century that women gained a measure of freedom in the matter of their own consent to the marriage.... The betrothal and the marriage were distinct legal proceedings among these tribes too.

PART II. THE DOUBLE TRANSITION AT THE CLOSE OF THE DARK AGES

In civil society the transition was in the social structures and cultures of the turbulent warrior-based communities of the Dark Ages to the more settled feudal societies of the Middle Ages.

In the institutional leadership of the Church, the transition was from its struggle to cope with the successive migrations and invasions in the West during the Dark Ages, to the assertion of its authority to control all aspects of political, social, economic and cultural life.

The transition in civil society

As the war-lords established their control over territories and their subject peoples they became more interested in their dynastic legitimacy. William the Conqueror got his revenge on those who taunted him about his status as a bastard by having their arms and legs cut off, and their torsos then thrown from the battlements. But what mattered was that he was the acknowledged son of his father, the Duke of Normandy, and was able and willing to defend the Duchy and extend his domains.

A generation later, the death of his son, Henry I, revealed a very different situation . Henry had several bastard sons, but his only legitimate heir was a woman. The result was many years of civil war. Everywhere in the West kings and nobles had to learn that the alternative to dynastic war was a set of fit male heirs. It was not enough to have an heir and a spare: several spares were needed. They all had to be male, and legitimate. A healthy bride was needed, preferably of the same status. But she was likely to give birth to as many daughters as sons and heirs.

Soon royal and noble households were full of virile young men, and nubile young women. Some of them could be betrothed at an early age, and eventually married off to secure alliances with other dynasties. The spare heirs, and most of the daughters were a problem. Allowing either to marry meant alienating property. So young men trained in the arts of war had to be kept on a short leash. Very soon they were rebelling against their fathers, demanding a role in government, with property, a bride, or all three. Duby gives many illustrations.

The daughters were in a similar predicament. They were not wanted in the numbers born, as it was their risk-embracing brothers who were likely to die young in military action. Some of them could be sent to convents, willingly or otherwise. The rest wanted a handsome husband and the role of his wife. But that meant alienating land as a dowry.

So there were soon numbers of princes and noble sons wanting attractive young ladies, and plenty of the latter willing to return the favour. As Duby (38-40) demonstrates, abductions and rapes took place on a large scale, many of the former with the enthusiastic cooperation of the ladies, and many of the 'rapes' probably consensual. Other abductions causing concern were those of widows holding large estates. The prohibition of abductions in the *Magna Ca*rta illustrates the concerns of the nobility at the time.

In these circumstances it became much more important for the legitimacy of births to be sustained by the validity of marriages. This required an accommodation with Church leaders, and as they too were in transition -from their weak defensive position in the Dark Ages to the dominance that they aspired to in the Middle Ages – there was room for new solutions that might satisfy both Church and State.

Church leaders' demands for power over the Emperor, kings and nobles were a reversion to their position in the closing years of Constantine, when they had secured for the clergy exemption from the criminal jurisdiction of Roman Law, an issue that led centuries later to the assassination of Becket, and is still with us today in the many attempts, all over the world, to protect paedophile priests from the criminal law. It is represented also by Hildebrand's attempts to undermine Henry IV, by excommunications and his humiliation at Canossa, and to the Investiture struggle. It is seen also in the forgery of documents – in particular the *Donation of Constantine,* and the *False Decretals* – to bolster the claims to power of Popes and Roman Curia. But these assertions of power were accompanied by rigorist views of marriage and sexuality. So the power struggle was accompanied by a theological struggle.

What the heads of royal and noble dynasties required in the feudal Middle Ages was a set of moral rules that protected them from rebellious sons and cousins, and another set of rules that would allow them to dispense with wives who proved infertile. The interplay of the modifications in these two sets of rules was concluded when the Middle Ages gave way to the Renaissance in the sixteenth century, with the second major rift in the unity of Christianity, the Reformation. The counter-Reformation of the Catholic Church at Trent led to the codification of the rules of marriage in the Catholic Church, and then to the internecine Thirty Years War in the seventeenth century.

Duby (1983: *passim*) shows how these two transitions were played out in Northern France. He also shows the concentration of Church leaders on the marriages of kings and nobles. They paid very little attention to the marriages of the peasantry. Had they done so they would have realised that the rules they laid down to determine the validity of royal and noble marriages would invalidate almost all the marriages of the rest of the community. For reasons that may be assessed as morally good or bad, Church leaders just wanted to control the politically powerful.

Schillebeeckx (1965: *passim*) demonstrates the readiness of the Church leadership to accept or negotiate the moral views and laws of a large number of Greek, Roman, Gallic, Celtic, Germanic, Frankish, Gothic, Anglo-Saxon and Viking societies, tribes and clans, most of which separated marriage into two parts: betrothal and formal marriage. He also (1965: 39-141) examines the liturgies and ecclesiastical rituals of marriage, sometimes non-existent, but greatly varied when they did exist. This erstwhile readiness to accept cultural variety suggests that Trent may not have said the last word, opening the door to a re-consideration of the relationship between betrothal and formal marriage.

The validity of marriages

Duby starts his account with the marriages of King Philip I of France. Having worked hard to purge the ecclesiastical hierarchy of simony in the choice of Church leaders, and immorality and the love of worldly pleasures – above all the love of women – Pope Urban II turned to deal with the laity, and make them pleasing to God.

In deep trouble himself, he launched the First Crusade at the Council of Clermont in 1095, and – among many other things – he excommunicated King Philip, for taking an additional wife, already married, while his own wife was still alive. In addition to this adultery he was accused of incest. What had shocked people was not bigamy, Duby (6) wrote:

> The trouble was that the woman he stole was related to him. She was not even related to him by blood; she was the wife of a very distant cousin, the great-grandfather of the count of Anjou being the great-great-grandfather of the king. But this was enough to bring down excommunication and anathema upon King Philip.

Refusing to give in, Philip was excommunicated again at the Council of Poitiers in 1099.

Philip had married Berthe de Frise when he was twenty. It was an arranged marriage (Duby: 7-8):

> His first cousin, the Count of Flanders, had given him her hand: she was his wife's daughter by a previous marriage. This … set the seal on a reconciliation between the king and his vassal and father-in-law.
>
> For nine years Berthe remained barren. But she prayed, and at last a son was born: Louis , later Louis VI. Despite this birth of Louis, Berthe was repudiated, though not until 1092, twenty years after her marriage….
>
> Philip's re-marriage caused a sensation ….all bore witness to ceremonies as solemn and holy as for a real marriage… The king, wishing the wedding to be an impressive occasion, summoned all the bishops to be present.

But Yves, the Bishop of Chartres, declined the invitation. Because of local anger at the interference of the Roman Curia, the metropolitan archbishop of Sens had refused to ordain Yves, who then got himself ordained by the Pope himself (Duby: 8-9).

> This was taken as an infringement of the powers of the king, and in 1091 the interloper was deposed by a synod. But Yves held out, relying on legates and on the Holy Father himself, insisting on the supremacy of papal decisions. Brought up as a rigorist, Yves was already inclined to sympathise with the reformers, and his present difficulties threw him into their camp.

Duby's account of this complicated saga continues for another twelve pages, Stressing again that all the documentary sources were prepared by churchmen, he contrasts the series of excommunications, condemnations and declarations by the Pope, legates, and councils with the fact that the bishops of Northern France were quite happy to attend Philip's second marriage, and annul his excommunication. (Duby: 16):

> The fact was that their moral values were different from those of the rigorists, and did not require their moving heaven and earth to separate Philip and Bertrade…. He held out for twelve years, keeping up appearances but never abandoning the woman he regarded not as his concubine but as his wife.

> …He was not giving way to senile passion but applying a set of moral standards. These rules were related to lineage; he was responsible for a patrimony…. In 1092 Philip had only one son, a boy of eleven. In those days eleven was a vulnerable age, and the child was delicate…. Philip could hope for no more children from Berthe; it was time for her to go….

Philip repudiated Berthe and married Bertrade. She bore him two sons and a daughter. Duby remarked (17):

> It was a good choice. At a time when the Capetian monarchy was much depleted, the king's first priority was to consolidate the reduced territory he was ruling as best he could from Paris and Orleans. The need was not to make brilliant alliances with great families of royal descent, but to lessen the power of the political groupings growing up around the chateaux of the Ile-de-France.

Eventually the War of the Investitures died down. In 1105 seven bishops met in Paris where the second marriage had been celebrated. Dressed as a penitent the king swore an oath: 'I will never again have relations or converse with this woman' ….Bertrade made a similar promise. So the anathema was lifted…. The two continued to live together …. (Duby: 13).

Provided the two new sons were accepted as legitimate Philip's kingdom was secure: Bertrade's brother held the key fortress at Montfort, and Bertrade was descended from Norman princes. But William Rufus was suspected of having designs on the French crown, and the security of the kingdom depended on acceptance of the second marriage as legitimate. Were Bertrade regarded as a concubine her sons would be bastards, and Philip's rivals could indulge in all sorts of hopes.

The development of Church rules about marriage

The Fathers of the Latin Rite inherited a deep repugnance for copulation and marriage. St Jerome, Duby (27) noted:

> had no doubt that Adam and Eve remained virgin in Paradise. So all marriages were accursed. The only justification of matrimony was that by bringing virgins into being it repopulated heaven…. But in itself marriage was evil. A husband was necessarily a fornicator and became an adulterer into the bargain if he came to love his wife with too much warmth. If that happened he also turned her into a prostitute.

Gregory the Great took up a similar position, but his influence was incomparably greater (Duby: 27-28):

> But though, like Jerome and Gregory, Augustine ranks husbands

> and wives a long way below the 'continent', at the bottom of the hierarchy of virtue, he does admit that man …still has the power to resist the encroachments of evil. He does this through marriage, the least imperfect form of copulation. The sexual act is a sin, but while it is mortal in fornication it becomes venial in marriage and can be redeemed.

In Carolingian France the bishops realised that the laity could not be led to virtue by inculcating a loathing of the married state (Duby: 30). So the Fathers were set aside and marriage was extolled as a possible framework for a good life. Emperor Louis the Pious gathered the leaders of the Frankish Church around him in 829. Their discussions led to eight propositions about marriage and the laity (*Petrologia Latine*, 162, cited in Duby (30-31):

1. 'The laity must know that marriage was instituted by God.'
2. 'There must be no marriage by reason of lust, but rather by reason of the desire for offspring'.
3. 'Virginity must be preserved until the nuptials'.
4. 'Men with wives must not have concubines'.
5. 'Laymen must know how to cherish their wives in chastity and honor them as they would any weaker being'.
6. 'A man must perform the sexual act with his wife not for pleasure but in order to beget children ….'
7. '… except in cases of fornication, a wife must not be set aside, but must be put up with; and those who having set aside one wife for fornication, take another, are held, according to Christ's words, to be adulterers'.
8. 'Christians must avoid incest'.

These, Duby (31) noted, could be reduced to three major precepts: monogamy, exogamy, and the repression of pleasure.

Jonas, Bishop of Orleans, elaborated on the eight propositions in a book, aimed at princes, cooperating with them in the maintenance of public order. Thirty years later, Duby (32) noted, public order was tottering. In Northern France the cultural revival was thriving, but the political order was crumbling. Concern about threats of violence led Hincmar, Archbishop of Reims to write books *On Divorce* and *On the Stamping Out of Abduction*. Arguing that the peace was being shattered by male greed and the desire to possess, the 'marriage pact' had to be restored, allowing women to be shared peacefully among men, and so to lend as much prestige as possible to the civil and secular rites by which this agreement was concluded.

There being then no religious rites the bond was forged (Duby: 33) in accordance with the 'laws of the world' and in accordance with 'human custom'. Duby's account echoes that of Schillebeeckx on marriage in the first century of Christian Rome.

Hincmar's emphasis on the crucial rites to be celebrated also echoes those described by Schillebeeckx in the first few centuries of Latin Christianity:

> the *desponsatio*, or the first stage of the matrimonial procedures, consisting of the agreement between the betrothed pair – or rather between their respective families (Duby: 33).

There were instances in Northern France at the time when priests were involved in marriage ceremonies. Hincmar himself had conducted the service of Judith, daughter of Charles the Bald in 856. But the Bishop of Bourges (Duby: 34) had forbidden his priests to take part in nuptial ceremonies. Only in the dioceses of Orleans and Bale were priests required to be present, even at the much more sober *desponsatio*. There was simply no marriage liturgy to accompany the civil rites.

Hincmar used the classical Roman tradition to define marriage:

> The *copula* of lawful marriage … is formed 'between two persons who are free and of equal rank … the free woman being given to the man by the decision of her father, dowered in accordance with the law, and honoured by public nuptials'. The union was completed by the *commixtio sexuum*, or the fusion of the sexes. There is no mention of prayers or of any kind of ecclesiastical participation (Duby: 34).

So matrimony was still relegated in Carolingian France to the margins of what was considered sacred.

The Dark Ages had seen a kind of tacit agreement between successive invaders and the Church. If the leaders of the former would embrace Christianity the Church would give them legitimacy. The bishops were concerned about in the maintenance of peace, and marriage was the foundation of public peace. This was difficult for the Church: after all, marriage was either evil (Jerome) or the lesser of two evils (Augustine and Gregory). The Church had had no part in this secular institution. It was not a sacrament (until the Council of Verona, 1184, the Second Council of Lyon, 1274, and the Council of Florence, 1439, decided that it was). There was no marriage liturgy, and no tradition of Church involvement – unless a cleric was getting married.

The sacralisation of marriage began with kingship. In the rite of coronation the presiding bishop underpinned the legitimacy of the king, and did so again in the coronation of his wife. The bishops now tried to add ethical content to the secular and traditional concept of marriage. They emphasised two of the rules: no divorce and a stricter interpretation of the incest taboo:

the prohibition of taking to wife a cousin within the seventh degree of consanguinity, or blood kinship, calculated in the Germanic manner (Duby: 35).

We have already seen that similar rules were applied to King Philip, following his marriage to Bertrade. This led to several excommunications, even though their relationship was one of affinity, not consanguinity. The seven degree Germanic rule was promulgated without explanation at the Council of Paris though contemporary scholars could find no basis for it. Leviticus was much less strict. The Roman law applied only to inheritance, and as it counted in both directions it barred only about a twentieth of the cousins now barred under the German rule.

Duby (36) noted that at the Council of Paris in 829

the prohibition was promulgated without explanation .... The second rule, requiring exogamy, was in outright contradiction of the first, which insisted on indissolubility. For a presumption of incest not only made divorce permissible, as in the case of fornication, but actually made it compulsory.

The Germanic seven degrees rule had a number of consequences. First, it effectively defined almost all marriages as invalid and incestuous. In the absence of genealogical records the peasantry had no way of knowing whether a particular couple intending to marry were blood relations within or without the seventh degree; the probability is that the overwhelming majority were within it. Second, it provided the Pope, the Roman Curia and individual bishops, with the possibility of threatening a particular king or noble, by suggesting that his marriage was incestuous and invalid. Third, it provided the king or noble who wanted to dismiss his wife, for any reason, with the explanation that he had now discovered that he had married, by mistake, someone now found to be related within the seventh degree of consanguinity. Fourth, it opened up the possibility, and often the necessity, of getting a Papal dispensation for marriage within the seven degrees, and post-facto legitimation of bastard children.

The decisions of the Council of Paris had momentous consequences. Their ambiguities, contradictions, and *ad hoc* solutions to pressing political needs, were to have disastrous consequences, such as the Hundred Years War between England and France, the English Wars of the Roses (or Cousins) and the decision of Henry VIII of England to wrest control of the Church in England, Wales and Ireland from the Papacy. The latter decision resulted in the majority of the population of England, North America, Australia and New Zealand today belonging to one or other of the Churches of the Reformation. The underlying causes and circumstances of these decisions of the Council of Paris will be considered in Chapter Six.

Kings and nobles had to maintain order in their domains. This requirement was seen in the political and military activities of rulers in the Carolingian period and later. Duby (38) noted that

> It was the duty of the king to pursue abductors in the same way as he pursued arsonists, murderers, or thieves. In feudal times, abduction was one of the four crimes involving blood law, a direct legacy of Carolingian royal justice. The sovereign, backed up by the bishops, was bound to put asunder couples who had not been joined together peacefully and in accordance with the prescribed rites. Such unions were not marriages, and it was necessary to dissolve them and to restore the kidnapped woman to the family from which she had been violently snatched. This had to be done so that the tissue of society should not be torn, so that the one initial disturbance should not through a concatenation of family feuds spread throughout the nobility.

The capitularies of the early ninth century demonstrate that the union of an abductor and his victim (or accomplice) was illegal (Duby: 38).

> If the girl was already promised to another man, that man was still entitled to take her and make her his lawful wife .... [But] if she had not already been previously been bestowed on another by the ceremony of the desponsatio, then all that was needed was her father's consent and a trifling penance, and the unlawfully formed couple could become a lawful husband and wife ....Marriage was a matter of free choice – not of the bride and groom, but of the bride's relations.

Dumezil had shown that there were four ways of taking a wife in Indo-European cultures. Two were ritualised, and two defied ritual. Duby (39) reduced these to two basic and contrasting forms:

> In one a girl is the subject of a legalised exchange, given by her father or bought by her husband, the transaction being carried out quite openly, ceremoniously, and with solemnities designed to uphold public order. In the other form the order is flouted and broken by a free and individual act that eludes all control: the girl gives herself to or is seized by the epic hero.

These contrasts can be seen not only in pre-Christian Indo-European cultures, in ninth century Northern France when it was in transition to a feudal society, but throughout the Middle Ages, the Renaissance and in twentieth century England and some American States. The eight propositions of the Council of Paris in 829 said nothing whatever about the consent of the two parties. When this became a condition of a valid marriage under Pope Alexander III the balance between Duby's two contrasting forms changed fundamentally.

The arrangements agreed by the bishops and the king in 829 were one set among many. Another report to Louis the Pious by the bishops in the same year drew on a model of marriage, the *connubium legitimum*, proclaimed by one of the Emperors, for consorts who were free and of equal status. But in the same texts the researchers, Duby (41) wrote

> found traces of another kind of union, also perfectly official but simpler and infinitely more widespread: concubinage. The Church had once regarded this very common kind of union as valid, giving it formal recognition in the year 398 in canon 17 of the Council of Toledo.

After all, the Emperor Constantine's mother, Helen, was a concubine.

> In 829 the Frankish bishops, while remaining intransigeant on monogamy, declaring that a man might have only one partner, were prepared to tolerate concubinage as a poor substitute for full marriage. They could hardly do otherwise if they did not want to destroy society. And there were advantages to this dual system. Precepts could be applied more flexibly. A priest might be refused a wife but allowed to keep a concubine. A noble might drop his concubine in order to contract a 'lawful marriage', and yet not commit bigamy. All that was needed was to quote another canonical text, a letter from Pope Leo I: 'A man who is married after having put away his concubine is not remarrying: the former was not a full marriage … not every woman united [*juncta*] to a man is his wife [*uxor*]. These words made it possible to leave custom undisturbed (Duby: 41).

Duby (41-3) refers to Frankish marriage laws that recognised three forms of union. In between

> the *Muntehe*, equivalent to the Roman 'lawful marriage', but far above a mere liaison, [was] the *Friedelehe*. This second-class kind of marriage was used to impose some discipline on the sexual actiivities of young men without involving family 'honor' in the long term…. A union entered into in this less definite manner was often temporary, but it was official, and was concluded by means of the appropriate rites….. The girl had been lent rather than given, but her relations had made the loan ceremonially, by contract, freely and in peace.

Charlemagne, for example, had lent his daughters in *Friedelehe.* Duby (42) notes that

> This flexibility in the matrimonial bond proved very useful over a long period. Written sources show concubinage of this kind to have been strongly established among the aristocracy of

northwestern France in the tenth and eleventh centuries. Perhaps the influx of the Scandinavians promoted its revival … it was referred to as marriage 'in the Danish manner'.

In the tenth and eleventh centuries the children of wives *more dan*ico were regarded as only second class heirs (Duby: 43).

The practice of concubinage lasted because it served family interests. It protected inheritances without … too openly thwarting the younger generation or … offending against the recognised secular system of values. … Such arrangements helped to keep the peace.

Duby (44) notes that the agreement setting up a concubinage was accompanied by rites, and that they were nothing like as elaborate as the betrothal and nuptials of a married couple. But he tells us nothing about them. He adds (Duby: 48) that

The Christianisation of marriage practices seems to have been effected easily enough in the lower strata of society, among people with few possessions and above all among those with none – the serfs, who did not even own their own bodies. Among the masses … the Church's version of marriage easily replaced the secular form of union, i.e. concubinage. Ninth –century inventories show peasants on large estates firmly paired off.

What he fails to note is that this 'Christianisation of marriage practices' left all the lower orders of society in 'marriages' that were invalid because they were incestuous as a result of the seven degrees rule. It did not replace concubinage; it preserved it in a new form from which they could not escape, while kings and nobles could escape unsatisfactory marriages by demonstrating that they were invalid under the seven degrees rule.

At the Council of Verona, 1184, at the Second Council of Lyon, 1274, and at the Council of Florence, 1439, the sacramental character of marriage was affirmed. But this did not end the centuries of dispute in the Latin Rite Church over this, and it was a major factor in the Reformation of the Sixteenth Century, with both Luther and Calvin disputing this.

More important in the cultures of Western Europe was the decree of Pope Alexander III that what made a marriage was the free mutual consent by the spouses themselves, not a decision by their parents or guardians. This, and later the *Decretum pro Armenis* issued by the Council of Florence, 1439, transformed the character of parental control in the culture of marriage in Western Europe. In England the *Paston Letters* and the records of Church courts reveal the tensions between parents who wanted to control their wayward daughter and the determination of the girl and her man to thwart them. The power of the girl's parents to decide her marital future could be nullified by her slipping away for a few minutes to meet the man she wanted to marry, so that they could exchange their vows in the presence of a witness.

PART III. THE EMERGENCE OF A CRISIS

Marriage since Trent

The canonical rules that defined a valid marriage at the Council of Trent are not dissimilar from those effective in the Churches of the Reformation for the next four centuries. But general acceptance that validity depended on free mutual consent, expressed in the presence of witnesses, utterly changed the dynamics. In twentieth century England - until 1940 - it was for the girl just a matter of getting to Gretna Green before her parents could stop her. If the parties were both over 21 they could until 2006 make a Common Law marriage in Scotland by exchanging consents.

Over eleven centuries successive interventions of the Latin Rite Church changed the ways men and women could get married. In the second half of the twentieth century the Catholic Church and the Churches of the Reformation finally lost their power to control the institution of marriage.

In the Dark Ages the institutional Church had been confronted by cultural change in the West which it had not understood, which it could not control, and over which its influence was minimal. Having built up powerful controls during the Middle Ages, over political institutions and over the culture of marriage, it proved unable to respond to the Renaissance, and failed to meet the challenges of the Reformation. The result was a century of conflict culminating in the Wars of Religion in the Seventeenth Century.

However, the Tridentine definition of marriage endured well into the twentieth century, for lack of alternatives. The Church of England set out in 1930 another view of sexuality in marriage, promptly condemned in *Casti Connubii.* In *Gaudium et Spes* the Church rejected the views of Jerome, Gregory the Great and Augustine that sexuality in marriage was an evil thing. The following year the Pontifical Commission offered a new approach for the Catholic Church, rejected outright two years later in *Humanae Vitae*. Instead of being 'received' the encyclical was itself rejected across the West, and in many parts of Africa and Asia.

Since the introduction of 'the Pill' in 1960 the sexually active population of the West has gone its own way, and most of the Catholic community has gone with it. The official teaching of the Church is increasingly seen as that of elderly celibate men who are utterly ignorant of the family of procreation, have never had to work for a living, never fathered a child or supported a wife and family. Worse, they are seen as ignorant of their own ignorance.

It is not unreasonable to assert that six decades ago a very high proportion of Catholics in England & Wales had no premarital sexual experience. Today premarital and extramarital sexual experience is the norm among Catholics. Six decades ago co-habitation was rare among twenties and thirties. Now it is the norm. Six decades ago promiscuity existed, but was rare. Now it is endemic, and taken for granted. In this situation the institutional Church can only deplore behaviour that is now treated as the cultural norm, deplore the ignorance of the young and middle-aged, and talk about God's forgiveness.

Finally, in this twenty-first century the State, in country after country, has simply re-defined marriage, so that legally it has ceased – for the first time in thousands of years – to have anything at all to do with human reproduction.

The outline of a solution

Why bother?

This book as a whole is aimed at suggesting practical solutions to three sets of problems arising out of human sexuality. The proposed solutions require a new and very different approach to preparation for marriage and family life, and on-going support for marriage and the family. This is outlined in Chapter Five.

This present chapter is focused on the development of solutions to one of the three sets of problems: premarital and extramarital sexuality, co-habitation, and promiscuity. It does so for several reasons. First, unregulated sexual behaviour, and promiscuity in particular, are very damaging to society, and to those who indulge in it. It is the source of much disease, and the spread of disease. When unwanted children are conceived it leads to abortion on an industrial scale. When the children are born their life chances are severely impaired, this being seen in educational outcomes, criminality, unemployment, poverty and a massive drain on the resources of the State and voluntary sector.

Second, the cohesion and stability of society depends to a considerable extent on the regulation of sexual behaviour. Societies, tribes, clans and communities have for many thousands of years regulated sexual activity in one way or another, because a measure of regulation is required for both social cohesion and the protection of social order. Two generations after the swinging sixties the wheel has come full circle. The last two decades have seen a moral panic over paedophilia that has now led to the present situation where many are so fearful of being denounced as sexual predators that they hold back from the simplest forms of kindness in public:

it is now often too dangerous to heed the Second Great Commandment without serious reflection.

Third, it is the source of much unhappiness and insecurity. In any society men, women and children need to know where the boundaries are. They may resent the restrictions that society places on them, and often try to circumvent them. But *anomie* in a society leads to deep unhappiness, and is well-known (cf Durkheim) as a cause of suicide and self-harm. This is particularly true in the area of gender relations and sexuality. When 'anything goes', as started in the Sixties, the first question had to be 'How far can I go?' But everyone had different answers. This led to much hurt and harm. Prior to the Sixties most Catholics would have paid attention to moral theology. But after *Humanae Vitae* moral theology as expounded by the institutional church lost its credibility. The huge, ecstatic crowds which idolised Pope John Paul II completely ignored what he said, and as soon as he left they carried on as they had before he arrived.

This uncertainty about the boundaries has affected both heterosexual and homosexual relationships. For decades teenage boys have competed with each other over what in earlier periods they might have called their 'conquests'. And teenage girls have for decades now been under pressure from the boys to 'have sex' with them. One result has been disturbing levels of teenage pregnancies. Another has been alarming levels of statutory rape of underage girls. And yet another has been the moral panic over 'inappropriate' behaviour by celebrities, high profile and costly trials, and the raising of the statutory bars and limits in order to define more 'inappropriate' behaviour as criminal. At the same time the law on statutory rape is seldom enforced, while another moral panic focuses on the statistics of rape, prosecutions and convictions.

The same has happened with homosexual behaviour. A collective sense of guilt about the legal persecution of Gays in the past has led to a general acceptance of homosexual behaviour, and the rights of Gays to enjoy the same liberties that heterosexuals proclaimed in the 1960s. Then another moral panic started, focused on celibate Catholic priests, the staffs of children's homes and boarding schools, celebrities and well-known politicians.

The foundations of a solution

This chapter has drawn heavily on two books for background information : Vol. II of Schillebeeckx' *Marriage: Secular Reality and Saving Mystery,* and Duby's *The Knight The Lady and The Priest.* The first systematically explores the development of the Church's official teaching on marriage up to the time of time of Vatican II, but we have followed it no further than the end of the Middle Ages The second examines in great detail what happened in Northern France between the ninth and thirteenth centuries, a microcosm of what was happening at different times and in different places in Western Europe as it moved out of the turbulent Dark Ages into the feudal Middle Ages.

The focus in this chapter has been on the practice and rituals of betrothal, and on the Church's attitude to extra-marital and pre-marital sexuality – in effect to 'fornication' and concubinage. This has been within a doctrinal framework where marriage started by being treated as an evil thing, and ended as a necessary institution that had been wrested from the control of secular society, tribes and clans, re-shaped by the Church, and kept firmly under its control – until the Swinging Sixties.

Pre-marital sexuality

In recent centuries fornication has been treated as mortally sinful by Church leaders. But it was not always so. In 862 the Third Council of Aachen declared that since chastity before marriage was rare and not expected, pre-marital sex was quite permissible. Duby (40-1) refers to the Roman Imperial code on the *connubium legitimum*, but the researchers found evidence of a

> perfectly official, but simpler and infinitely more widespread kind of union, concubinage. The Church had regarded this very common kind of union as valid, giving it formal recognition in the year 398 in canon 17 of the Council of Toledo.
>
> In 829 the Frankish bishops … were prepared to tolerate concubinage as a poor substitute for full marriage. They could hardly do otherwise if they did not want to destroy society. And there were advantages to this dual system…. A priest might be refused a wife but allowed to keep a concubine…. All that was needed was to quote … a letter from Pope Leo I: 'A man who is married after having put away his concubine is not remarrying: the former was not a full marriage … not every woman united to a man is his wife. These words made it possible to leave custom undisturbed.

The *Decretum* of Bishop Bourchard of Worms, prepared between 1007 and 1012, was a carefully arranged guide to himself on the gravity of sins and their appropriate penances. It was copied on a wide scale and used extensively in Germany, Italy, Lotharingia and Northern France, until superseded by Gratian's (Duby: 61-62). It includes the questionnaire to be completed in each parish by seven men prior to a visitation:

> Eighty-eight transgressions were set out in descending order of gravity…. The first fourteen questions relate to murder …But immediately after this category, the second rank, came the twenty-three questions … dealing with marriage and fornication….

> A decreasing scale of guilt emerges: guiltiest of all is the married man who takes the wife of another; next comes a man who keeps a concubine in his house....Last in this part of the list, and very venial because it was so frequent an occurrence in large houses filled with chambermaids, is the dalliance indulged in by young men and single women.

The penances to be prescribed by confessors likewise indicate the view that some sexual offences – such as solitary masturbation, and the fornication of an unmarried man with a woman with no marital ties, or with his own maidservant – merited the very mildest of penances, ten days on bread and water (Duby: 67). The penances to be awarded depended very much on whether the man was married. This reflected the widespread recognition (Duby: 68) that marriage had two aspects: one concerned with the sexual and the other with social morality. The married man who fondled a woman's breasts got five days fasting; the bachelor got away with only two days.

By the end of the eleventh century the Church reformers had essentially won the struggle against the Nicolaitans which (Duby: 116-7) was essentially the fight against married priests:

> At the beginning of the eleventh century, amid the great turmoil from which new powers were emerging, the prelates' great preoccupation was to try to save the monopoly, privileges and immunities as servants of God .... [priests] must be kept well away from women. If the clerics ... were to preserve the hierarchy that subordinated the laity to the clergy, they had to establish a sexual distinction between men, with some of them consigned to perpetual chastity....
>
> The battle was already waging in 1031 ... when the Council of Bourges excluded the sons of priests from religious orders, forbade young women to be given in marriage to priests or deacons or the sons of either, and barred anyone from marrying the daughter of a priest's or deacon's 'wife'.

At the Council of Rome in 1069, Duby (118) noted,

> the canon issued by the Council of Toledo in 398 insisting on monogamy – but leaving the choice between marriage and concubinage open – was quoted once more. After that, however, it is never mentioned again in official documents. From then on the leaders of the Church, while expelling marriage from its own fold, began to aim at trapping the whole of the laity in a net in which each mesh was a duly consecrated marriage. There were to be no more free unions, no more couples living on the fringe

In the last decade of the century the 'Gregorians' won (Duby: 117-8):

> The main casualty of this long struggle was concubinage, the half-measure between the two extremes. The bitterness of the battle had led Gerard of Cambrai to advocate the simplest solution: the *viri ecclesiastici* should have no female partner at all, lawful or otherwise, while the *viri seculari*, who needed a female partner, must have a lawful wife. No physical union was allowed outside the *connubium legitimum*, solemnly entered into by both religious and secular rites.

The penalties for pre-marital sexual intercourse continued to vary greatly from place to place and time to time. In England the *Paston Letters* mention the public whipping of a couple for fornication – not just a few days of penance on bread and water – the man having already been whipped publicly seven times. Yet until the Hardwicke Marriage Act of 1753 sexual intercourse after betrothal was as lawful in the Anglican Church as after marriage. In Scotland marriage by co-habitation and repute did not end until 2006.

The details of what constituted *connubium legitum* were not finally spelled out until Trent, but for eight and a half centuries the laity more or less toed the line, in the Churches of the Reformation as well as in the Latin Rite Church. Over the last half century the Latin Rite has seen large numbers of its secular priests quit the priesthood, because of their unwillingness to tolerate any longer the decisions made in the late eleventh century, leaving the laity unable to hear Mass or receive the Eucharist in large parts of many dioceses. The determination of the centralisers, the rigorists, the Gregorians in the late eleventh century, to imbed the clericalisation of the Church that had begun under Constantine, had disastrous consequences in the sixteenth and seventeenth centuries, splitting Christianity for the second time. Since the middle of the twentieth century it has split Latin Rite Christianity itself, with massive defections and - in the West - a new unwillingness of both laity and clergy to accept doctrinal statements of the Pope, the Roman Curia and the bishops.

PART IV. TOWARDS A SOLUTION

A suggested solution with three elements

The growth of unregulated sexual behaviour in the sixties and seventies has done immense damage in many societies in both the West and the Third World, to social structures as well as cultures. The early history of the Latin Rite Catholic Church provides a model that should now be considered in the twenty-first century. The Council of Toledo in 398, insisted on monogamy, but left open a choice between marriage and concubinage. The canon was still being quoted 671 years later at the Council of Rome in 1069.

Effectively the young and the middle-aged in the West – Catholics, other Christians and many with no religious affiliation - have for half a century, like the bishops at Toledo and at the Council of Rome in 1069, seen marriage and co-habitation as alternatives. The first element in a solution is for the institutional church to recognise this.

The second element in a solution is to go back to the experience of marriage over several millennia in Indo-European societies, to the history of Christianity in its first millennium, and to recognise betrothal, engagement, the affirmation of an intention to marry, as a critically important stage in the process of getting married, and restore it to its former dignity, and social as well as religious significance.

The third element in a solution is to recognise marriage as a process that begins with friendship, followed by courtship, recognised publicly at betrothal and concluded and celebrated at marriage. The betrothed couple would then be recognised at betrothal by both the institutional Church and the civil community as in the first stage of marriage, expected to enjoy sexual intercourse - **but on one condition**, that they use effective contraceptive measures to ensure that no child is conceived until they are formally married.

Preparation, rituals and social controls

Relationship education, from age three to old age, is dealt with in Chapter Five, suggesting how children, adolescents and young adults should be prepared for marriage and the creation, support, nurture and socialising of a Christian family. There it is suggested that courtship should be marked with the social acceptance by parents, relatives and friends that the couple are now boyfriend and girlfriend, and are withdrawing to some extent from their wider circles of heterosexual relationships to concentrate on each other.

Early in the courtship the two sets of parents, and the Christian community, might use rituals like those found in Roman, Greek, Celtic, Frankish and Germanic societies. Boyfriend and girlfriend could exchange rings made of a base metal, in the presence of their parents, when they were ready to declare their new relationship. Relationship education, at home and at school, would have made it clear that tentative kissing and discreet intimate touching - by mutual consent - were now permissible, but two-timing was not, and that sexual intercourse was very definitely not allowed.

Well before betrothal, relationship education in secondary school and at home, would have stressed the significance of the public declaration of the couple that they **intended** to get married, that they **intended** to commit themselves to each other in marriage. In modern Western societies they might find it very difficult to **make** that commitment at marriage itself for some time, because contemporary culture expects couples to have at the time of marriage what their grandparents only came to enjoy after several or many years.

Cultural change in the West has imposed on young couples developments - which they have widely accepted - that are delaying marrying and child-bearing well into their thirties. Relationship education at school, in the family and within the Church, would have encouraged adolescents to put to one side the pressures of advertisers and the peer group that demand an expensive wedding – not just a shared meal after the exchange of their vows, but a full day to impress the guests, even two days, with costly entertainments, perhaps abroad.

Both pre-marital sexual relationships and co-habitation are now very widely accepted as moral behaviour in the West, by Catholics, other Christians and those with nor religious beliefs and affiliations. In accepting betrothal as the first stage of marriage the Church would be encouraging its members to support betrothed couples and help them to prepare for marriage and the creation of a family.

When finally the betrothed couple are ready to get married, they would be expected to announce this publicly, and the man expected to present his future bride with an engagement ring that he could reasonably afford.

CHAPTER THREE

THE FUNCTIONS OF SEXUALITY IN MARRIAGE AND THE OBLIGATIONS OF RESPONSIBLE PARENTHOOD

SUMMARY

The present chasm between the beliefs of the People of God and those of their institutional leaders represents for Latin Rite Catholicism a catastrophe almost as great as the Reformation – almost, because it has led to no wars, civil wars or other violence. Its underlying cause, discussed in Chapter Six, is 'cultural lag'.

The Natural Law argument relied on to condemn contraception in Humanae Vitae is flawed, and fails to convince the laity, for a number of different reasons. The institutional leadership of the Latin Rite has been focused on the 'purpose' of marital sexuality, which it defines as procreation, while the experience of the laity leads to their being focused on 'function'. The leadership has been unable to justify its argument that in modern society procreation is the primary purpose of sexuality in marriage. Their critics point to a fundamental difference between the nature of humanity and that of the other primates, a difference emphasised by the Christian belief that we are made in the image and likeness of God. For the laity the primary function of sexuality in marriage is to sustain the bond of affection between husband and wife, which is the foundation of the family.

Experience of family life occure in two phases, first in the family of orientation and then in the family of procreation. Laity and Latin Rite clergy and bishops all experience the first, but only the laity experience the latter. Oriental Rite Catholic and Orthodox clergy experience both, as do the clergy of the Churches of the Reformation. But Latin Rite clergy and bishops are ignorant of the family of procreation. They have not had the experience of getting and holding a job, feeding, housing and socialising children, or had to cope with the dilemmas of responsible parenthood.

The clerical elite have perceptions of the Great Commandments quite different from the laity. The are focused on the First, while the laity are focused on the Second, on love of neighbour, and the nearest neighbour is wife or husband. They lack too the emergent understanding of marital sexual union as the holy communion of marriage, analogous to the Holy Communion with Christ in the Eucharist. That holy communion of marriage not only sustains the married couple during their struggle to bring up a family, but it creates the emotional bond that helps them to care for and nurse each other in the disabilities of old age and dementia. Elderly bishops know nothing of this.

Responsible parenthood has to cope with dilemmas at both family and societal level. Contemporary Western societies largely cope with those at family level through societal interventions and birth control. The modal British couple in their seventies today is incomparably better off than two centuries ago.

At societal level there remain problems. Casti Connubii delayed the reductions in birth rates in mainly Catholic countries, but Humanae Vitae did not, as the faithful rejected it and have largely ignored it. The failure in social responsibility has been in the rich and powerful ignoring the Second Great Commandment and taking effective control over a high proportion of both GDP and societal wealth in many countries.

The 'pastoral approach' adopted by bishops in many countries may have eased the consciences of many Catholics, but it seems to have had little or no effect on Catholic fertility. With crude birth rates falling across the world, Catholic fertility fell much faster. In Canada the ***relative*** *fertility quotient fell 41% between 1971 and 2007, from 1.15 to 0.68. In the Philippines it fell 25%, from 1.40 in 1971 to 1.05 in 2007. In that year it was the only one in sixteen populous states with a quotient above 1.00.*

The newly-elected Bishop of Rome quickly demonstrated that he had a very new view of episcopal pomp and circumstance, in Rome and elsewhere, a new attitude to those he met, especially the poor and afflicted. But he made it clear that his basic theological outlook was that of his three predecessors. He offered a new solution to what all four saw as sin, God's mercy. However, for the majority who have defied Humanae Vitae the problem is not their alleged sin but the blindness of popes, prelates and the Roman Curia to their own personal ignorance of marital sexuality. They ask not for God's mercy but for a dialogue between the institutional leadership and the theologically informed leaders of the laity, who have what the bishops do not have – personal experience of marital sexuality and the family of procreation.

The solution suggested in this chapter has two starting points. First, Humanae Vitae is not part of the Church's doctrine. It was not 'received' by the faithful; it was vigorously rejected, and is now effectively ignored. Second, even if Humanae Vitae were part of the Church's doctrine, it is 'reformable', just like many earlier doctrines, once accepted, now rejected.

The first step in the suggested solution is the drafting of a new statement of the moral theology of sexuality in marriage, reminding all of the assertion in Vatican II that sexual intercourse in marriage is good in itself. The second would be an assertion that couples must accept moral responsibility as parents for supporting and socialising their children. The third would be be an insistence that they alone are morally responsible for the size and spacing of their family, and for the means they choose.

PART I. DIFFERENT PERSPECTIVES

Introduction

The encyclical *Humanae Vitae* in 1968 opened up, very publicly, a rift in the Catholic Church, between the majority of the People of God who dissented from it and the leadership of the Church which either proclaimed it or accepted it. The growth of this rift is examined in some detail in Chapter One. It can be summarised by observing that the Catholic nuptiality rate worldwide (i.e. Catholics married with the rites of the Church, per thousand Catholic population) had been 11.8 in 1970, and had fallen to 4.4 in 2011. Marriage had played a major part in the Reformation of the Sixteenth Century. The present rift between the beliefs of the faithful and those of their institutional leaders represents for Latin Rite Catholicism a catastrophe as great as the Reformation.

What caused the rift?

The underlying causes are examined in detail in Chapter Six. For present purposes we can simply assert that the fundamental cause – since Vatican II, just as in the sixteenth century – has been 'cultural lag'. Over two millennia the cultures of the world, and those of the People of God living in the world, have changed continuously. But the institutional leadership of the Catholic Church has neither 'monitored' these changes – observing and considering them as they happened – or adapted their message to respond to them. Instead, the institutional leadership has generally condemned them and opposed them. Pope John XXIII was one of the few who expressed the need for an *aggiornamento* in the Church. It is not yet clear whether Francis Bergoglio shares the understanding of Pope John XXIII that the Church must embrace the modern world, as the Council recognised in *Lumen Gentium* and *Gaudium et Spes*, or whether he wants to apply the salve of God's mercy to a People of God so invincingly ignorant that they are unable to recognise the truth in the prescriptions and proscriptions of the institutional leadership.

Knowledge, perceptions, personal experience

There are very basic cognitive differences between the institutional leadership of the Latin Rite Church and the laity. These can best be understood if the morality of contraception as a means of regulating births is studied under six heads:

(i) the Natural Law;

(ii) perceptions and the failure of the Natural Law debate;

(iii) function v purpose;
(iv) experience of family life;
(v) different perceptions of the two Great Commandments, and
(vi) theology of sexual intercourse in marriage.

The Natural Law

A few points can usefully be made now. First, in *Casti Connubii* Pope Pius XI condemned the use of the 'safe period' as well as 'artificial' contraception. Pope Pius XII, however, took a different view, and set in motion a variety of attempts to establish morally licit procedures that couples could use to ensure that the wife did not conceive a child. Moralists do not seem to have appreciated that confining marital sexual intercourse to the safe period meant that it was **not** open to the transmission of life. The whole point of confining it to the safe period was to ensure that there was **no** transmission of life.

Second, the last link with Revelation was severed by the dropping of the argument about the Sin of Onan. Henceforth, the official position was based exclusively on Greek philosophy, updated by Augustine and Aquinas.

Third, while the official exposition of Natural Law recognised the importance of Man's (and Woman's) ability to think and reason, it did not appreciate the implications of the human capacity to learn and remember, immeasurably greater than that of other species.

Fourth, the official position simply asserted the primacy of reproduction as the 'purpose' of sexual intercourse, without justifying that assertion. This will be considered further below.

Fifth, the official exposition took no account of the statistics of ejaculation. Many **millions** of sperm are ejaculated during intercourse. Sometimes, **one** will result in a conception, and in exceptional circumstances more than one. Nature ensures that there is no openness to life for all the other millions.

Sixth, far from being 'received', the assertions made about the Natural Law were massively rejected by the People of God when *Humanae Vitae* was published in 1968. Their behaviour, as the Church's official statistics have shown (in Chapter One), has been increasingly dismissive of the Natural Law argument since 1968, not just in the West but in other continents.

Seventh, the relevance of Natural Law rather than Positive Law is widely disputed. The former admits no exceptions, but the latter recognises a hierarchy of values, *epikeia*. *Pace* Kaiser (1987: 165), the Common Law of the Anglophone cultures not only permits *epikeia* but demands it when a higher order value is threatened by a lower one.

Different perceptions and the failure of the Natural Law debate

There seem to be as many different perceptions of the Natural Law as there are exponents of it. None, it seems, can convince the critics that the Church has any valid claim to speak with authority on what is in effect a pagan Greek system of thought, given a Christian veneer by Aquinas.

When the Natural Law argument was tested in repeated debates by the members of the Pontifical Commission the American Jesuit theologian, Ford, who had been most adamant in arguing that it established that contraception was gravely sinful, was obliged to confess that he could not demonstrate his argument (McClury: 111.)

Purpose v function

The Latin Rite institutional leadership of the Church have had a fixation on purpose, giving overriding priority to procreation. To many of the People of God there is something quite bizarre about the presumption of men who have no personal experience of marital sexuality telling those who have such experience what its purpose is.

Those who do have personal experience of marital sexuality recognise procreation as its secondary function in modern society. A healthy couple, married in their early twenties, will have sexual intercourse some four or five thousand times during their life together – very different from the rest of the animal kingdom. They don't need this to 'increase and multiply', but to sustain the marital bond[10]. That bond is good in itself, as an expression of love, but it is essential for the well-being of the family, and the raising, nurturing and socialising of children. Again, this is because Man's (and Woman's) nature is very different from that of other species. Unlike the rest of the animal kingdom human offspring take a long time to mature - physically, sexually, mentally and emotionally. They need loving parents throughout infancy, childhood and adolescence. The female menopause ends the woman's reproductive life at about the time when her daughters need her help in raising her grandchildren.

The reason why the human species takes so long to mature is that we have a capacity that is denied to all other species. Our brains give us an incomparable capacity to think, to reason, and to learn and remember. Well-educated Christians have no difficulty in embracing Darwinian theories of evolution, and later developments about the role of mutations in DNA. But they do not see the human species as a rather superior development of the chimpanzee. They take seriously the teaching of Jesus that we are made in the image and likeness of God, and that we are temples of the holy spirit. Above all, it is the very essence of our nature that we think, reason, learn and remember.

---

[10] See Davis, quoted in Kaiser (1987: 144-5).

In this perspective the primary function of sexuality in marriage is to sustain the bond of affection between husband and wife. That bond – not a 'contract', with a marital 'debt' that has to be 'paid' – sustains their love, their trust in each other, their determination to create and maintain a loving, caring, responsible environment for their children. Their responsibility, as spouses and as parents, is to be prudent in both the spacing of their children and the number. They, not Popes, Roman Curia and the Episcopal College, have to feed, clothe, house, educate and socialise their children. And thinking Christians, whose nature it is to reason, learn and remember, will also have some regard to the impact of their own reproduction on the communities and societies in which they live, and on the well-being of humanity as a whole.

Experience of family life

Human beings experience family life in two phases. As infants, children and adolescents they experience and learn about the family of orientation. They gradually move from total dependency on their parents to the independence of the young man/woman who has successfully emerged from the storm of adolescence. This is the common experience of almost all humanity, whatever their beliefs, of both the Latin Rite laity and those who go on to develop clerical roles within the institutional church.

The overwhelming majority of the laity, and of those who develop clerical roles in the Oriental Rites of the Catholic Church, in the Orthodox Churches, and in the Churches of the Reformation, go on to marry and develop a family of procreation. The only two groups within the People of God who have no experience[11] of procreation are those who freely accepted celibacy on entering a religious order – Catholic, Orthodox or Anglican – and those who accepted celibacy as a condition of ordination in the Latin Rite secular priesthood. And it is the latter, when later given episcopal ordination, who have asserted their authority to make rules for marriage and the family of procreation – an institution and a social group of which they have no personal experience or knowledge whatever[12]. This is not 'the blind leading the blind', but 'the blind misleading the keen-sighted'. This is considered further in Chapter Six.

Different perceptions of the two Great Commandments

This too is considered in more detail in Chapter Six, as one of the consequences of the clericalisation of the Church that began under

---

[11] Miniscule numbers of Latin Rite secular priests are trained and ordained after being widowed. In the Anglophone world the Latin Rite priesthood now includes significant numbers of married priests, formerly Anglicans.

[12] Addressing the Council, Maximos IV, the Melkite Patriarch, spoke of a 'celibate psychosis' (Kaiser, 1987: 180-1).

Constantine. This clericalisation was halted, even reversed, during the *volkerwanderung* of the so-called Dark Ages, but it was resumed at the start of the Middle Ages, in the ninth and tenth centuries.

One theological feature of this clericalisation was the gradual focus of the clerical leadership on the First Great Commandment. More and more attention, time and thought was give to sacramental matters, rituals, rubrics, vestments and sacred buildings – and much less attention to the Second Great Commandment, 'to love one another, as I have loved you'.

The laity, however, have generally, over two millennia, focused on the Second Great Commandment. They usually know their close neighbours well. They sometimes find it difficult to love some of them, but they know that they must go on trying to do so. They are also aware of Jesus' insistence that the Samaritan too, culturally and socially very different, must be loved, and they often find this very difficult indeed. Not experiencing the closeness to God of the clerical elite, the laity often find it easier to express their love of God by loving their neighbours. And the neighbour closest to them is husband or wife

Theology of sexual intercourse in marriage

The Roman Curia has never published the report of the Pontifical Commission on Births, but it was leaked by Idoc in April, 1967. The metre-high stack of the twelve bound volumes of evidence submitted to the Commission has likewise been kept secret. But a steady trickle of books later in the twentieth century has provided a detailed account of what happened when the Commission was sitting, and subsequently.

A further important development was the emergence of a lay Magisterium, as more and more of the laity – especially women – got university degrees in theology, and then started teaching it at universities. The clerical elite not only lost its monopoly of theological learning but soon found that professorial chairs were being filled by lay men and women able and willing to contest the statements and rulings of the clerical elite.

One aspect of this was the emergence of an understanding of sexual intercourse as the holy communion of marriage, analogous to the Holy Communion with Christ in the Eucharist[13]. Husband and wife express their love for each other in sexual intercourse. It sustains their marital union, and in so doing it emotionally strengthens the family within which they nurture and socialise their children. It strengthens the bond between husband and wife so that – their family grown up, and flown the nest – they

[13] I put this to a Jesuit in 1949-50, when I had no personal experience at all of sexual intercourse – in or out of marriage. He did not respond. Kaiser (1987: 184) quotes a similar remark by Colette Potvin, a member of the Commission. Jack Dominian, and Kelly (1982: 60) have made similar suggestions.

can care for each other in the infirmities of old age. Just as elderly Latin Rite bishops have no experience of the family of procreation, they have none of caring for and nursing a wife with dementia[14].

The damage done to their union, and so to their family, by constant preoccupation with limiting sexual intercourse to the 'safe period', was described in detail in the evidence to the Commission of the Christian Family Movement. It showed that Catholic couples trying very hard to respect the prescriptions and proscriptions of the Church leadership, were torn between their duty of responsible parenthood and obedience to the clerical elite, who had no personal experience whatever of the burden they were imposing on good Catholic couples.

PART II
OBLIGATIONS OF RESPONSIBLE PARENTHOOD

For many thousands of years families and societies have encountered dilemmas in procreation. The dilemmas are, however, different at family and societal level.

The dilemma at family level

This arose as a consequence of high mortality rates in all societies prior to the development of scientific medicine. The source of the family income – a smallholding, a farm, or a craft workshop – depended for its continuation on couples having enough children surviving to maturity to run it, and support their parents once the latter were too old to work. As infants, children and adolescents died before reaching maturity, they had to be replaced. This meant great strain for the wife and mother. Failure to produce enough mature offspring to run the enterprise meant losing it. A high crude birth rate was essential for survival.

The dilemma at societal level

However, an imbalance could emerge quite quickly between high birth rate and high death rate. Wars, pestilence and natural disasters could reduce the population of a society over a short period, exposing it to predatory societies.

Societies could become predatory as a result of the ambitions and lust for power and riches of their leaders. But they could also arise as a result of overpopulation, due to the sustaining of a high birth rate during a

[14] One of the most appreciated speeches about marriage at Vatican II was that of the Melkite Patriarch of Antioch, cited above, many or most of whose priests were married (Kaiser, 1997: 97-8)

period of peace, benign environmental conditions, or good government that reduced the death rate.

When overpopulation emerged, particularly in migrant communities and hunter-gatherer societies, it resulted in the invasion of territories occupied by neighbouring societies. So the *volkerwanderung* of the Dark Ages arose from population pressures in the East that pushed tribes and clans to the West. Overpopulation, like the lust for power and riches among leading elites, led to aggression and war – and still does today, as societies seek land, water and other natural resources.

Solutions to these dilemmas

Since the Enlightenment three cultural developments have emerged that together have been, and are, creating solutions. The first is a series of economic revolutions based on science – in agriculture, industry, commerce, transport, communications and finance. These have raised productivity right across the world, so that almost all societies today have levels of productivity and income far higher than in the last third of the seventeenth century.

The second is the emergence of new political philosophies that emphasise human dignity and rights, the accountability of leaders to the led, and systems of international law designed for the peaceful resolution of conflicts between states, and rules to limit the suffering and damage caused by warfare. Not all the philosophies of the Enlightenment have been so benign. A few have given rise to militarism and nationalism, but they are the exception, and two world wars have revealed the suffering they cause.

The third is the application of science to medicine, resulting in extraordinary improvements in the expectation of life at birth. They have continued apace since World War II, so that in almost all countries expectation of life has increased dramatically over the last six decades. Scientific medicine continues to improve both personal health and community health. Not all are willing to exercise the self-discipline needed to benefit from modern knowledge of personal and social medicine, but overall the improvements have been remarkable.

Obstacles to these solutions

The societal benefits of these three solutions are not found uniformly in all countries. The benefits are distorted by the lust for power and riches in leadership elites that ignore human dignity and rights, are unaccountable, and defy international law. Then endemic corruption in some societies – even those that have embraced the political philosophies of the Enlightenment – has undermined their capacity to produce goods and services, and has allowed the corrupt in effect to steal from the poor.

Again, even in societies that respect the rights and dignity of their citizens, and constantly seek out and suppress corruption, there are wide and growing disparities between the incomes and assets of their elites and those of the poor. Those who vote in elections in Western societies that have inherited Christian beliefs and values often seem to have forgotten the Second Great Commandment.

It is sometime asserted that one of the main obstacles to these solutions is the teaching of the institutional leadership of the Church expressed in *Humanae Vitae*. It is clear that, during the three decades between *Casti Connubii* and Pope John XXIII's appointment of the Pontifical Commission on Births, the prescriptions and proscriptions of Church leadership hampered in many countries a reduction in birth rates *pari passu* with the reduction in death rates.

But it is also clear that by 1962 the international community was no longer prepared to tolerate Vatican opposition to programmes of birth control. That was the rationale of the appointment of the Commission. The leaking of the news of its appointment changed for many the status of both *Casti Connubii* and the relaxations of Pope Pius XII. Now it was *in dubium*, and *libertas* followed. The leaking of the report of the Commission settled the matter for massive numbers of Catholics: the moral quality of contraceptive birth regulation was no longer *in dubium*. Then *Humanae Vitae* was not 'received': it was rejected across the world. Episcopal Conferences were too frightened of the Roman Curia to demand an Extraordinary Synod. As theological literacy among the laity increased more and more of them not only ignored *Humanae Vitae* but saw it as theologically in error.

In 1968, faced with vigorous protests across the world, individual bishops and Episcopal Conferences adopted a 'pastoral approach'. Most of the laity were seen as 'invincibly ignorant'; they were using contraceptives because they could not understand; leave them in peace; 'don't ask, and don't tell'. The difficulty with this pastoral approach was that it was the Pope and the Roman Curia who were seen as invincibly ignorant, lacking the personal experience of the family of procreation that the laity had.

The failure of the pastoral approach

Table 1B, derived from the *Statistical Yearbook of the Church*, demonstrates the failure of *Humanae Vitae* to affect the marital sexuality of the faithful, 1970-2011. At world level Catholic child baptisms per thousand Catholic population fell from 24.1 in 1971 to 11.6 in 2011, i.e. by 51.9%. Tables 3A and 3B reveal the extraordinary scale of the laity's rejection of *Humanae Vitae*. With the exception of Germany there were catastrophic falls in the Catholic child baptismal rates between 1971 and 2008. But that is a spurious exception: in 1971 the German rate was already below the 2008 rate in almost half of the other countries listed.

Table 3B summarises the available crude birth rates of the most populous states in the world in the world, 1950-2011. As there are so many gaps in the data it is difficult to compare most of its figures with the baptismal rates in Table 3A. But an attempt is made to do this in Table 7, where the relative fertility quotient is, for each year and each state, the Catholic child baptismal rate divided by the corresponding crude birth rate.

Often cited as two of the three most fervently Catholic nations, the Netherlands and Poland both had a quotient close to unity in 1971. Poland's rate remained remarkably stable for four decades. This demonstrated that although Poland's Catholic baptismal rate dropped by 36% between 1971 and 2008, in defiance of *Humanae Vitae*, all children born to Catholic

Table 7. Catholic relative fertility quotients in the most populous states, 1971-2008

N. America	**1971**	**1995**	**2001**	**2006**	**2007**	**2008**
Canada	1.15	1.02	0.87	0.72	0.68	...
USA	1.28	1.19	1.11	0.94	0.95	...
S. America						
Argentina	...	0.90	0.84	0.78	0.76	...
Peru	0.72	0.47	0.46	...	...	...
Venezuela	0.75	0.68	0.73	0.66	0.67	...
Asia						
India	...	0.67	...	0.69	0.71	0.71
Japan	0.93	1.19	0.97	0.76	0.76	0.76
Korea, South	...	0.74	0.64	1.04	0.50	0.51
Philippines	1.40	0.95	...	1.13	1.05	...
Europe						
France	0.85	0.68	0.62	0.54	0.54	0.53
Germany	0.69	0.93	0.86	0.84	0.83	0.84
Hungary	1.66	0.70	0.78	0.88	0.90	0.89
Italy	1.00	0.93	0.88	0.82	0.80	0.80
Netherlands	1.06	0.58	0.65	0.59	0.55	0.56
Poland	0.96	1.05	1.03	0.97	0.97	1.03
Romania	...	0.42	0.59	0.57	0.59	0.60
Spain	1.03	0.91	0.81	0.68	0.69	0.69

parents were baptised. In the Netherlands the baptismal rate fell 66%, and the relative fertility quotient nearly halved. Not only were Catholic couples defying three Popes, the Roman Curia and the Episcopal College by regulating their own fertility, a high proportion were so alienated from the institutional church that they made no use of the baptismal rites of the Church. Having no other way to express their views, they voted with their feet, as the Dutch figures in Table 4 confirm. For the previously enthusiastic Dutch Church *Humanae Vitae* was a pastoral and evangelistic disaster.

In 1971 Catholic relative fertility was well below unity in Peru, Venezuela, France and Germany. Catholic couples were not only defying the teaching of the institutional church, but many of them were already so alienated that they were not using the baptismal rites of passage for the children born to them. Only in Hungary, the Philippines, the USA and Canada were the Catholic quotients markedly above unity. The Hungarian quotient fell 46% between 1971 and 2008 when it was well below unity, suggesting that significant numbers of Catholic parents were not getting a Catholic baptism for their children.

In the Philippines the baptismal rate fell 44% between 1971 and 2008. In both years it was above the Asian figure. The Philippines quotient fell 25% between 1971 and 2007, when it was still a little above unity. The implication is that in 1971 its Catholic population had a fertility well above that of the population as a whole. Then defiance of *Humanae Vitae* greatly reduced the difference, but in 2007 Philippino Catholic parents were still using the rites of the Church for baptism.

In Canada the Catholic child baptismal rate fell 61% between 1971 and 2008, as Catholic parents emphatically rejected the official teaching of the institutional church. The quotient fell 41% between 1971 and 2007, from Catholic fertility well above the national norm in 1971, to near unity in 1995, and then continued to fall rapidly to well below unity in 2001 and later years. By 2007 the quotients imply that something like a third of the children born to Catholic couples were not being baptised.

In the USA the Catholic child baptismal rate fell 39% between 1971 and 2008. In 1971 the Catholic quotient was 1.28, indicating fertility well above that of Americans as a whole. But between 2001 and 2006 the quotient fell below unity, implying that significant numbers of Catholic parents were no longer ready to have their children baptised.

The Catholic quotients for 2007 show that in only one of the sixteen countries, the Philippines, was the quotient above unity. In all the others it ranged from 0.50 (South Korea) to 0.97 (Poland). The stridency of the encyclical *Humanae Vitae* itself was a total failure, and so was the 'pastoral' approach adopted in many countries.

However, if *Humanae Vitae* had no discernible effect on the already declining birth rate it probably delayed in some countries the decline in the death rate. The institutional church did not apply the 'pastoral' approach in countries ravaged by HIV/AIDS, and tried hard to weaken the resolve of some governments and legislatures to promote the use of contraceptives to protect adults from HIV/AIDS. It also prevented Caritas organisations from cooperating in their supply and distribution. Effectively the institutional leadership of the Church promoted not 'openness to life' but 'openness to death'.

The new approach of Francis Bergoglio

The newly-elected Bishop of Rome demonstrated from the start that he is a very different person from his three predecessors. First, his style is very different. He immediately made quite clear his refusal to live in the isolation, extravagance and pomp of earlier Popes.

Second, he established himself as being pastorally very different from his predecessors, but nonetheless theologically of the same mind as his three predecessors about the issues that concern the laity. Like all the other bishops appointed since 1978 he endorsed the teaching in *Humanae Vitae.*

Third, he revealed an important strand in his thinking in his criticisms of clericalism, an issue discussed at some length in both Chapter One and Chapter Six. But he has still to explain the grounds of his criticism or to elaborate on it.

Fourth, over and over again he stressed God's mercy for sinners, allowing many to see this as a way out of the theological positions that separate him as an orthodox theologian from most of the People of God. It seems that People of God, in their ignorance, still do not understand the unchanging teaching of the institutional leadership on the evils of contraception, cohabitation, re-marriage after divorce, etc. But they can be re-assured: God will be merciful to them.

However, there is a problem for moral theology here. Is it rational for the laity to seek God's mercy when they have not sinned, either objectively or subjectively, by using contraceptives? For many among the People of God there is no doubt that sin – grave sin – is involved, but they see it is the structural sin of the institutional leadership of the Church, in insisting on a teaching which is not the teaching of the Church, because it has not been 'received', but instead was massively rejected. Many among the better-informed laity, in their franker moments, would agree with little hesitation that there is a great need for God's mercy in the Church, starting right at the top with Popes and prelates, cardinals and curia, who have misled the People of God for a millennium and a half, lusted for power and ignored the Second Great Commandment. At the bottom of the pile there must be many of the laity who have not had the moral courage to protest at the evil perpetrated at the top, and many among the lower clergy who have obediently held their tongues.[15]

[15] The author needs God's mercy for failing to protest publicly at the conspiracy - of Cardinal Godfrey and Archbishop McQuaid of Dublin in 1960 - to suppress the report that the

The laity, the overwhelming majority of the People of God, do not seem to be asking for God's mercy on the grounds that they are ignorant sinners who persist in the use of contraceptives. What they are asking for is a dialogue between

(i) the institutional leadership, who are ignorant of the functions of sexuality in marriage, because they have **no** personal experience of the family of procreation, and

(ii) theologically informed leaders of the laity who **do** have that personal experience.

Following such a dialogue the People of God would be asking for an intellectually honest attempt to re-state the official position of the institutional leadership that acknowledges

(i) the functions of marital sexuality, and

(ii) the moral obligations of married couples to exercise social responsibility in their sexual life, both in relation to their own families and to their stewardship of the natural environment.

This should lead into an intellectually honest study of structural sin within the institutional church, which

(i) began with Constantine's exemption of the clergy from the criminal courts of the Roman Empire,

(ii) set in motion the clericalisation of the Church, suspended or in retreat during the Dark Ages, resumed in the early Middle Ages, and seen in the lust for power epitomised in the humiliation of the Holy Roman Emperor at Canossa, and the punishment of Henry II at Canterbury after the murder of Becket – a determination to hang onto power still manifest in the institutional church today in all the attempts of the Roman Curia to ensure that paedophile priests are protected from the State's criminal justice system – an issue discussed in some detail in Chapter Six.

Finally, this dialogue should lead to an intellectually honest review of the institutional church's attempts, over a millennium and a half, to present its official teaching as an unchanging reflection of Divine Revelation – an issue again discussed further below, and in Chapter Six.

International Catholic Migration Commission (ICMC) had requested, responding to the expressed concerns of Cardinal Mimmi, a report the present author had himself drafted, on the *Integration of Irish Immigrants in England & Wales*. It was eventually published by the Irish Manuscripts Commission in 2012, half a century too late. See Chapter Six.

PART III. A SOLUTION IN OUTLINE

The extent of the problem

The bishops assembling in the Extraordinary Synod on the Family, in October, 2014, did not cause the crisis, though the timidity of many of them - in failing to carry out their collegial responsibilities by challenging the Roman Curia, and in allowing the continuing clericalisation and centralisation of the Church – prolonged and deepened it.

The consequences of the failures of the Episcopal College over six decades to challenge the Roman Curia have been illustrated in a number of statistical tables relating to child baptisms, marriages and Mass attendance. The Church is in a crisis today potentially as severe as that in the Renaissance, which precipitated the Reformation

Two starting points

The first is that *Humanae Vitae* is not part of the Church's doctrine. It was not 'received' by the People of God. In fact it was vigorously rejected. The grounds for that rejection were set out in the report of the Commission on Births.

The second is that even if *Humanae Vitae* were part of the moral theology of the Church it would be 'reformable'. Over a millennium or more the institutional leadership has asserted that the moral teaching of the Church has been and always will be unchanging. In fact it has not only 'developed' in the manner Newman demonstrated, but it has in many matters been abandoned, and in a few it has been turned upside down. Slavery is now condemned, though at the start of the nineteenth century the Papal States were still using slaves to power their galleys[16]. The payment of interest was condemned as usury. Heretics and witches were burnt alive – for their own good. Crusades against the Arabs were promoted or supported. Anti-Semitism was still enshrined in the Holy Week liturgy at the time of Vatican II. Unbelievers were persecuted and/or forced to convert. The death penalty was approved and used, as was torture. The suppression of colonial peoples was approved, and the castration of choirboys. The Syllabus of Errors was promulgated, and then overturned in less than a century. *Extra Ecclesiam Nulla Salus* was re-interpreted into oblivion. No one now endorses Jerome's condemnation of sexual intercourse in marriage. The acceptance of Gregory's and Augustine's denigration of sexual intercourse within marriage, as a most regrettable necessity that had to be tolerated, continued until it was overturned at Vatican II. The views of Jerome, Gregory and Augustine on women are now rejected even by conservative

---

[F]For an account of the institutional church's treatment of slavery from St Paul to 1965, see Kaufman (1995: 46-9)

theologians. 'Mixed education' – allowing Non-Catholics and Catholics to be educated together – was forbidden, but is now enthusiastically applauded by institutional leaders. The 'co-education' of boys and girls was condemned but has been the norm for well over a century. Marriage was not a sacrament, until four Councils declared that it was. The validity of a marriage depended on the consent of the fathers of the couple, until Pope Alexander III decided that it depended on the free consent of the couple themselves. Pope Pius XII corrected the teaching of Pope Eugene IV and the Council of Florence on the 'matter' of the Sacrament of Orders. Infallibility of the ordinary, universal Magisterium has never been defined, and has been taught only since 1862.

Catholics who are theologically less literate have little awareness of the above 'developments' in the doctrines of the Church. Generally they have taken place over a long period of time, usually by the gradual accumulation of conditions, qualifications, provisos and exceptions. But sometimes they have been quietly abandoned, so that only the diligence of historians like Noonan has revealed the curious way that many of the changes in the 'immutable' doctrines of the Church have occurred. Now that the Magisterium includes large numbers of lay professors of theology it will be much more difficult for the Roman Curia to defend doctrines on the basis that they are part of the irreformable teaching of the Church.

A way ahead

In the absence of a General Council it is open to the Extraordinary Synod on the Family and the Ordinary Synod of 2015 to draft a new statement of the moral theology of sexuality in marriage. The first step would be a reminder of the assertion in *Gaudium et Spes* that sexual intercourse in marriage is good in itself, as an expression of the love of the husband and wife for each other. This could be strengthened by recognising it as the holy communion of marriage, analogous to the Holy Communion of the faithful with Christ in the Eucharist.

The second step would be to assert the need for couples to be morally responsible parents, recognising that they must ensure that physically, socially, emotionally and financially they can support, nurture and socialise the children they procreate. And rich couples would be reminded that extravagant use of natural resources within the family would be as much a sin against the Second Great Commandment as neglect of their offspring.

The third step would be to insist that parents, and parents alone, are morally responsible for decisions about the size and spacing of their families, i.e. for birth regulation, and also for the means they use. Such decisions must be based on an 'informed conscience'.

For a long time the institutional leadership of the Church has presented the 'informed conscience' as the conscience that has obediently accepted the rules laid down by the legitimate leaders of the Church, i.e. themselves. It is in effect a conscience that has, under obedience, been handed over to the leadership. This interpretation of conscience has had a dreadful history in world affairs. In the name of obedience to legitimate leaders untold millions have been murdered, societies have been destroyed and civilisations wrecked. The repeated interpretation of 'informed conscience' in this way has stained the reputation of the Church for centuries. It has been a major factor in the current crisis over paedophilia, as bishops and superiors have been ordered by the Roman Curia to refrain from informing State authorities about abusive priests, and have obeyed. This is considered further in Chapter Six.

Moral theologians have offered a very different view of an informed conscience. First, a conscience decision is based on human reason. Second, it must be free, neither coerced nor prompted by a duty of obedience to authority. Third, it is based on personally accepted moral principles and values. Finally, it is based on the facts of the situation, including their social context. Only the particular married couple can know the relevant facts of their situation and their social context. Celibate bishops are ignorant in general of the realities of marital sexuality because they have no personal experience of the family of procreation. And no prolonged questioning in the confessional can help priests to discern the relevant facts of the particular couple, because they too lack any personal experience of the family of procreation.

Conclusion

Humanae Vitae has done immense damage to the married lives of countless good Catholic couples, and has grievously harmed the Church. It is now generally ignored by the majority of good Catholics, though some still have scruples about their defiance of the Roman Curia. The damage done to the Church can be seen in the falls in Catholic baptismal rates and the falling Mass attendance rates.

This situation has persisted for four and a half decades because individual bishops and Episcopal Conferences have been too timid to challenge the centralised power of the clerical elite of the Church, the Roman Curia[17]. The Church now has in Francis Bergoglio a Bishop of Rome who seems to be anxious to curb the clericalism that began under

[17] Cf Suenens on bishops who for decades had not studied the pros and cons of *Casti Connubii*. They received directives, they bowed to them, and then tried to explain them to their congregations (Kaiser, 1987: 216-217).

Constantine, to end the centralisation that reached its zenith at Vatican I, and to put into practice the Episcopal Collegiality proclaimed at Vatican II.

These proposals represent a way out of the current crisis within the Latin Rite Catholic Church over sexuality in marriage, which threatens a catastrophe as great as that of the Reformation in the sixteenth century.

CHAPTER FOUR. MARITAL BREAKDOWN IN THE TWENTY-FIRST CENTURY. A REVIEW AND SOME PROPOSALS

SUMMARY

It took the Church a millennium and a half to decide in 1439 that marriages were indissoluble. It had taken it a millennium for it to take an interest in marriage generally. Apart from royal and noble families, the Church was content to leave the regulation and celebration of marriage to local tribal and clan communities.

The attempt to control marriage began under Constantine, but was halted by the incursions of the Dark Ages. The clericalisation of marriage was resumed in the Early Middle Ages, marked by the declaration at the Synod of Verona in 1184 that marriage was a sacrament. The gradual assertion of control over marriage was accompanied by an equally gradual enforcement of clerical celibacy.

Social distance between the clerical elite and the laity was gradually increased, and left the former either unaware of or opposed to the social changes that were transforming the lives of the laity. This cultural lag had explosive consequences in the Sixteenth Century. Refusal to accommodate the need of the English King Henry VIII for a male heir led to his seizing control of the Church in England and Wales, and as a result Catholics were in a small minority among the colonisers of North America and Australasia.

Trent remedied one aspect of cultural lag, the poor education of many of the clergy, but the remedy exacerbated clericalism and the social distance between the laity and the clerical elite. Centuries later Pope John XXIII recognised the need for an aggiornamento, but once the bishops had left Rome the Roman Curia re-asserted its power and persuaded Pope Paul VI to issue Humanae Vitae. It proved a pyrrhic victory as the People of God rejected it.

Social and cultural change has accelerated since 1965, especially in relation to human sexuality, marriage and family life, which the institutional leadership has vigorously criticised, but not attempted to accommodate – until the decision in 2013 to summon the Extraordinary Synod on the Family.

The Church produces no statistical data on the breakdown of Catholic marriages, but some inferences can be drawn from a statistical measure, the Catholic relative nuptiality quotient. In fourteen populous states in 1971 only three had a quotient above 1.00, indicating a Catholic nuptiality rate higher than that in the state as a whole. In 2007 the quotient was well below 1.00 in sixteen states. In Canada the quotient fell by 71% between 1971 and 2008, in Peru by 56%, in France by 52%, and in the Netherlands by 73%.

The background to these figures is a general reluctance to get married in a large number of societies. But the failure of baptised Catholics to use the rites of the Church is far greater. It reflects both a rapidly declining demand for the Church's rites of marriage and a rapidly declining supply of those rites, from institutional leaders opposed to re-marriage after divorce.

Understanding of the permanence and indissolubility of marriage has been transformed by the widespread civil legislation permitting and facilitating divorce. But couples considering divorce often have little idea of the damage it does to their children. Nor do they usually appreciate how messy and expensive divorce can be. But for children the breaking-up of co-habiting parents is usually even more damaging than divorce.

Meanwhile, the ubiquity of divorce, and much later ages at marriage, make it much more difficult for someone to find a suitable spouse who is neither divorced nor co-habiting. At the same time the bureaucratic legalism of the institutional Church is difficult to reconcile with either justice or the Second Great Commandment. It would be far better for large numbers of Catholics if they had avoided a canonical marriage with the rites of the Church. Other systemjs of law, like the Common Law of the Anglophone world are far less rigid, and more nuanced. Above all, they allow contracts between two parties to be ended by mutual consent. The clerics who manage the Church's annulment system seem to have no understanding of the damage it does to both the parties and their children.

The suggested solution is very simple. The ubiquity of divorce makes it probable that most marriages between Catholics are basically invalid, because one or the other of the parties had conscious or sub-conscious reservations about permanence and indissolubility. The institutional Church should recognise a presumption that when a marriage has manifestly failed it was invalid at the start. Such a presumption is not new. Under the seven degrees rule in the Middle Ages almost all marriages – outside royal and noble families – must have been invalid, but the institutional Church presumed them to be valid. The only parties who could prove invalidity were the royal and noble families – and the bishops, when they wanted to create difficulties for political leaders.

Were the institutional Church minded to do something more positive than the suggested presumption of invalidity. It might set up systems and programmes to help couples to lead good, fulfilling, happy and productive lives, to identify marriages that were failing, and try to support them.

In the event of marital failure and divorce the Church's primary aim should be to minimise the hurt and harm suffered by the children. It should seek to investigate failing marriages, request the co-operation of the parties to protect their children, and allow admission to the Eucharist only to the parent(s) co-operating, and continuing to co-operate after re-marriage.

PART I. BACKGROUND AND DEVELOPMENT OF THE PROBLEM

Introduction

The Church's present official position, that marriages are indissoluble, was declared at the Council of Florence in 1439. It had taken almost a millennium and a half to reach it, and it has been much questioned since Vatican II. The words of Jesus on the indissolubility of marriage, often quoted, are well known – but their meaning and implications have been much debated[18].

What is not really questioned is that the institutional church was very slow to take an interest in marriage generally (Duby, 1984). It was regarded for many centuries as a most regrettable necessity for the survival of humanity. Apart from royal and noble marriages the Church left it to local tribal and clan communities to regulate and celebrate it. Royal and noble marriages were the exception because bishops were well aware of the dreadful consequences for peace and prosperity of dynastic rivalries such as the Hundred Years War between England and France, and the English Wars of the Roses (or Cousins). They also saw control of marriage as a useful tool in exerting power over royal and noble families

The Church's assumption of control over marriage

This began under Constantine, when the elite status of the clergy was marked by their exemption from the criminal jurisdiction of Roman Law, a matter further discussed in Chapter Six. For Romans it could be handled under Roman Law, which still underpins the law of much of continental Europe. But it was not so easy for Greeks. Then the *Volkerwanderung* of the Dark Ages, and the collapse of the Roman Empire in the West, halted both the clericalisation of the Church and the general application of Roman Law to Christian marriage in the West. Not until the advent of the early Middle Ages in the tenth century was the clericalisation process resumed, and the gradual assertion of centralised clerical control over marriage. The first marker in this process was the declaration, after

---

[18] Kelly (1982: 19-63); Kaufman (1995: 103-132)

centuries of denial, of the Council of Verona in 1184 that marriage was a sacrament. This, and the problem of indissolubility, were major factors in the Reformation of the sixteenth century.

Social distance between clergy and laity

In the Latin Rite Church another important development occurred during the Middle Ages, the requirement of celibacy among the secular clergy. This was gradually enforced, so that between the tenth and the thirteenth centuries the secular clergy (and the bishops) became a clericalised quasi-caste, increasingly distant from the laity.

This created new problems. The later Middle Ages and the Renaissance brought rapid social change to the West. Via the Islamic Arab Middle East, via Syrian Christian translators and Moorish kingdoms in El Andalus, scholars of the Holy Roman Empire came to learn of the literature of Classical Greece. And they learnt too about the principles of Roman Law, lost in Rome itself as it was ravaged by Germanic invaders. The Renaissance was a new cultural flowering in the West, in art, architecture, literature, science, technology and governance. It brought widespread social as well as cultural change.

The laity and their rulers were in their daily lives well aware of the positive and negative aspects of this social and cultural change. But their increasingly clericalised and centralised elite were not. The adaptations required of the Church to this change were not made. They were resisted. Creative innovators were not heeded; they were punished, often burnt at the stake. The result was the explosive Reformation that split the Church in the North and West, ushered in wars and civil wars that continued into the middle of the seventeenth century, and to this day has profoundly affected Christianity in the West as the conflicts were taken by colonisers into the New World, Africa and Oceania.

Trent remedied some of the cultural lag, for example in the training of the secular clergy. But this particular remedy accentuated the social distance between clergy and laity. Some issues were not dealt with at all, such as the use of the vernacular. Cultural lag continued to grow, and was accentuated by the accelerated centralisation that happened after Vatican II.

Pope John XXIII was sensitive to this cultural lag. He recognised the need for an *aggiornamento*, and summoned Vatican II. In five sessions the Council tackled a wide variety of issues, but Pope Paul VI reserved to himself two highly contentious issues, contraception and clerical celibacy. The Roman Curia saw no need for a Council, tried to control it at the very start, failed, but came back before it ended in an attempt to regain control. Soon it succeeded, and its victory in persuading the Pope to reject the report of the Pontifical Commission on Births, and issue *Humanae Vitae* in 1968, has marked the following four and a half decades.

However, *Humanae Vitae* proved to be a pyrrhic victory as it evoked not 'reception' but furious rejection by the People of God across the world. Since Vatican II the Roman Curia has managed to suppress episcopal collegiality, and has continued the clericalisation and centralisation of the Latin Rite Church. Few individual bishops, and no Episcopal Conferences, have had the moral courage to challenge the Roman Curia.

Alienation and ignorance of marriage and sexuality

The cultural lag has accelerated since the bishops left Rome in 1965. Technological change has revolutionised communications and the economy, and cultural change has led to an extraordinary proliferation of new styles of family life, challenges to the *mores* of sexual behaviour and rapid alienation among the People of God, who now often have no respect for or trust in the institutional leadership of the Latin Rite Church. This alienation is manifested in falling Mass attendance rates, but above all in falling baptism rates and falling nuptiality rates among the People of God. A sociologist can find plenty of evidence for thinking that the Latin Rite Catholic Church is on the brink of a catastrophe as great as the Reformation.

The continuing scandal of priestly paedophilia is just one of many indicators that the centralised and clericalised elite of the Latin Rite Church is so out of touch with social and cultural change among the People of God that it just cannot understand what all the fuss is about.

Among the laity the last four and a half decades have seen a huge growth in the numbers of laymen – and particularly laywomen – who have got university degrees in theology, have begun to teach theology in universities and are now members of the Magisterium, as holders of university chairs in theology, and quite capable of disputing with the clerical elite.

There is now a wide chasm of misunderstanding between the Latin Rite clerical elite, who seem oblivious to the alienation of the People of God in general, and unaware of their own personal ignorance of the institution of marriage, an ignorance that arises from their never having experienced the family of procreation.

The crisis of marital breakdown

Since *Humanae Vitae* the Catholic nuptiality rate – the number of Catholics married with the rites of the Church per thousand Catholic population – has fallen dramatically. This cannot be attributed to *Humanae Vitae* itself, but to the institutional shurch's official position on divorce, and remarriage after divorce. Not surprisingly, the *Statistical Yearbook of the*

Church does not publish data on marital breakdown in the Catholic population. But it is possible to make some inferences if we compute Catholic relative nuptiality quotients for the most populous states. These are derived from Tables 2A and 2B, and are set out in Table 8. They are the result of dividing the Catholic nuptiality rate, for each state and each year for which data is available, by the total nuptiality rate for the same state and year.

Table 8. Catholic relative nuptiality quotients in the most populous states, 1971-2008

State	1971	2001	2006	2007	2008
N. America					
Canada	1.05	0.45	0.34	0.30	0.30
Mexico	0.79	0.62	0.59	0.56	0.57
USA	0.58	0.40	0.34	0.34	0.33
S. America					
Argentina	...	0.57	0.56	0.51	...
Peru	1.26	...	0.53	0.48	0.55
Venezuela	0.48	0.36	0.27	0.37	...
Asia					
Japan	0.82	0.49	0.35	0.35	0.33
Korea, South	...	0.66	0.62	0.58	0.55
Europe					
France	0.85	0.49	0.42	0.40	0.41
Germany	0.67	0.36	0.34	0.34	0.34
Hungary	0.69	0.29	0.40	0.43	0.41
Italy	1.03	0.83	0.77	0.80	0.71
Netherlands	0.91	0.40	0.28	0.28	0.25
Poland	0.87	0.86	0.78	0.75	...
Romania	0.67	0.45	0.39	0.36	0.41
Spain	0.97	0.80	0.60	0.59	0.62

In only one of the countries in Table 8, Peru, was the 1971 quotient markedly above unity. In Canada, Italy and Spain it was close to unity. In Peru the Catholic nuptiality rate fell 60% between 1971 and 2008. Following legislation on divorce its relative nuptiality quotient fell 56% as Catholics divorced and re-married like the rest of the population.

In Canada the Catholic nuptiality rate fell 84% between 1971 and 2008, while the quotient fell by 71%. In Italy the Catholic nuptiality rate fell 61%, while the quotient fell only 31%. In all other countries the quotient was already below unity in 1971, the lowest being 0.48 in Venezuela. In

2008 the quotient was down to 0.25 in the Netherlands, 0.30 in Canada, and 0.33 in the USA and Japan.

When marriages failed the overwhelming majority of Catholics were not prepared to go through the long, opaque and elaborate nullity procedure, and were not prepared to tell their children that they were bastards because their parents had never been married – notwithstanding the evidence of all the wedding photos. The institutional church had added insult to incomprehension, injustice and unconcern, and massive numbers of Catholics in failed marriages just walked away.

In the Western world, where marriage is increasingly rejected, why are Catholics apparently rejecting marriage so much more emphatically than their fellow citizens? They are not. Apart from Catholics who share the widespread disenchantment with marriage as an institution they are as likely as their fellow citizens to re-marry after a divorce, and to seek marriage with a divorced person – but not with Catholic rites, as the institutional church will not provide them. So they either marry with civil rites or with those of another Christian Church. In retrospect many divorced Catholics might reflect that it would have been far better to have entered into a canonically invalid marriage in the first place. If they are theologically literate they might recall that the sacrament of marriage is conferred by the bride and groom on each other, as the priest is merely a witness.

There is not one crisis but several. Understanding of the permanence and indissolubility of marriage since Vatican II has been transformed by massive recourse to divorce, following widespread legislation permitting and facilitating divorce. Divorce in many cases is followed by re-marriage. When first married couples make the required vows about permanence but they all know that they can end their marital status quickly if they so wish. They may be quite sincere in their pledges at the time, but they know that society will not hold them to account if they break them.

Unfortunately, couples considering divorce often have little idea of the damage that marital breakdown inflicts on their children. Irrespective of their age, almost all children suffer as a result of the ending of their parents' marriage. In terms of the outcomes for children in later life there is a clear gradient between the best and the worst: continued family life with two married parents is best, followed by continued life with two unmarried, co-habiting parents, followed by living with one parent in a successful marriage, followed by living with a single divorced parent, and finally with a single parent, never-married.

Not only do parents not appreciate this gradient to failure, but those who start in marriage seldom understand how messy, painful and expensive divorce is, and the difficulties that have to be faced in getting financial support from the parent who does not have custody. The problem of support is even worse when there is no divorce, because the parents were not married, and worst of all when the child was conceived outside co-habitation, following a casual encounter.

The ubiquity of divorce in the West, combined with a gradually rising age at (first) marriage, and increasing co-habitation, has another consequence. A man or woman seeking a suitable person to marry encounters increasing difficulty in finding someone who has never married and is not already co-habiting. The West has seen a massive growth of information systems that aim to help those seeking a spouse or partner, sometimes through advertising in printed media but increasingly on websites. There is a large marriage market, but it is quite different from the markets that existed a century ago, based on local communities and family networks. There are huge numbers of people seeking a spouse or partner, but a high proportion of those they find have already been married and divorced, or are co-habiting.

Roman Law and the legalism of the clerical elite

The evidence that marital breakdown is highly damaging to the children of the union is incontrovertible, but so too is the evidence of the damaging consequences of the institutional church's bureaucratic legalism. Instead of obeying the Second Great Commandment and trying to express love for the parents and children, the institutional leadership is emphatic: if the tribunals do not grant an annulment the marriage continues to exist so long as both parties are still living, the Church will neither celebrate or recognise another marriage, and any Catholic who enters into another marriage in such circumstances will be barred from the Eucharist. This rigidity arose from the re-discovery of Roman Law in the twelfth century (Winter, 2002: 8), brushing aside what was in effect the *epikeia* of the Dark Ages.

In this clear-cut situation the behaviour of the two parties before and after the divorce are seen as canonically quite irrelevant. The consequences of this can be seen from a quick summary of three cases:

(1) Happily married couple. Wife wants children, but does not conceive. Eventually it is established that her husband is sterile as a result of mumps. Wife divorces husband, without rancour. Husband late in life wants to marry a childless woman already past the menopause. But he has already been told never to darken the door of the church again if he re-marries. Enters a civil marriage, and the couple have some years of happiness before she is diagnosed with Alzheimers. He cares for her and nurses her for ten years until she has to be admitted to a nursing home. He then spends several hours every day with her, feeding her, talking to her, and generally caring for her, until her death. A moral

theologian might see sin in this account, but would it be the sin of a loving husband cast out of the Catholic community, or the structural sin of an institution so obsessed with legalism that it has totally lost sight of the Second Great Commandment? But the clerical leadership hasn't finished yet. The old man cannot be re-admitted to the Eucharist until he has given a full account of his sins to the Church's representative, expressed his sorrow, received absolution – and carried out his penance.

(2) Wealthy Catholic couple, happily married. Husband an industrialist, and chairman of an important lay Catholic organisation. Needs marital intercourse. Contraception not allowed. Half a dozen children born in quick succession Wife exhausted. Husband turns his attentions to his secretary, who accompanies him on travels, and has no inhibitions about contraception. Divorce follows. Years later wife marries again. Refuses to brand her children as bastards by seeking an annulment. Joins them at Mass but cannot receive Holy Communion with them. And, of course, is 'living in sin', committing adultery.

(3) Catholic couple, well-rooted in the Catholic community, with five children, who have four first cousins, and two first cousins once removed. All have been married. First child (now grandmother) could not marry with Catholic rites as husband, a Catholic, had been divorced. He abused three children and wife, who eventually divorced him. She now cohabits. Cannot marry with Catholic rites because partner too has been divorced. Goes to Mass every Sunday, is a reader and receives Holy Communion. Couple's second child married with Catholic rites. Character difficulties emerged: her husband had been child of a very unhappy marriage. Divorces him. Declares that she is now an atheist. Co-habitation followed by civil marriage. Third child rejected Catholicism in his teens. Married with Anglican rites. Declares that he is an atheist. Very happily married, and successful professional, husband and father. Children unbaptised. Fourth child wanted to marry with Catholic rites, but her husband had been divorced. PP refused even a 'blessing'. Married with Methodist rites. Daughter unbaptised. Fifth child wanted an Anglican country wedding. Persuaded to have the family 'chaplain' as Church's witness, but now alienated from the Church and has two young children unbaptised. Two of children's first cousins married without Catholic rites. One cohabited with man who fathered two children, and much later left them. All alienated from the Catholic Church. One of the couple's two much older first cousins married, with Catholic rites, a well-educated Catholic man, who fathered three children and then found someone else he preferred. Marriage ended with divorce. Wife unable to re-marry with Catholic rites. Her brother was to have been married with Catholic rites but at

the last minute his bride refused. Alienated from the Catholic Church. Very happily married. Successful professional, husband and father.

What emerges from the above cases is that most of the marriages were wrecked or put in jeopardy by the prescriptions and proscriptions of the institutional leadership of the Latin Rite Church, who have no personal experience whatever of the family of procreation and marital sexuality. It would have been far better if **all** of those involved had married with the rites of another Christian Church, fully understanding that it is **they** who confer the sacrament of marriage on each other. Their bitterness, misery and alienation would have been avoided. And in those cases where the marriage collapsed they would have been quite free to enter into another marriage without agonising about exclusion from the Eucharist. The cases cited above, and the extraordinary fall in Catholic nuptiality rates, suggest that in the Latin Rite huge numbers of the faithful in the West have realised that the best solution is to avoid altogether the rites of marriage of the Catholic Church.

How did the institutional leadership of the Church come up with these rules governing marriage? There is no evidence of them in the Gospels. The Roman Army was occupying the country when Jesus was teaching, but his only reference to Roman Law related to Caesar's head on the coinage. Roman Law became involved only because it was the legal basis of marriage in Rome at the time of Constantine. It was a ready-made system allowing the new clerical elite to increase its control. It was lost during the Dark Ages, and then re-discovered in the early Middle Ages – and once more came to be used to re-establish the clerical leadership's control over the laity.

Other systems of law, like the Common Law used in most of the Anglophone world, are far more nuanced; they provide for conditions and qualifications, and the termination of contracts by agreement. If a person contracts to sell a house to another, and it is burnt down before completion of the contract, then the contract is ended. He/she will be expected to deliver to the other party the proceeds of the insurance. If he/she contracts to supply goods or services to another and finds that it is quite impossible to do so, because of an earthquake or an armed invasion, he/she can plead *force majeure*. The other party can then go to arbitration. If the terms of the contract create insuperable difficulties there may be legislation prohibiting 'unfair' terms. In exceptional circumstances the common good may lead to legislation changing the law to deal with the difficulties. What is common to many of these examples is the importance of delivery. If the two parties agree to terminate the contract, they are free to do so. If they cannot agree the terms for ending the contract, they can go to arbitration or seek remedies in the courts.

Annulment

The institutional Church's approach to marital breakdown is utterly dysfunctional for both the couples involved and society in general. It also defies the Second Great Commandment. It is difficult to find any trace of love in it. It completely ignores issues of justice. One party to the marriage may have acted impeccably, and the other abominably, but no distinction is made between them. The contract cannot be ended – and continues to exist - so long as both of them are alive. Only if sufficient grounds can be found for annulment can either party marry again with the rites of the Church, and be admitted to the Eucharist.

The rules and procedures of annulment involve massive delays. The clerical leadership, with no personal knowledge of the family of procreation, and no experience of marital sexuality, demonstrates in case after case that it is quite unable to empathise with those seeking a declaration of nullity. Neither do the clerics involved seem to understand the consequences for family morale and solidarity of declaring that the marriage never existed, so that all the children are bastards.

PART II. A SUGGESTED PRAGMATIC SOLUTION

The outline of a solution

Kelly (1982*: passim*) offers a comprehensive, nuanced approach to the issue of indissolubility in Jesus' lifetime, and the issue in our very different modern Western world. He invokes Kuhn's (1962) work on paradigmatic shift and argues that the 'contract' pattern of marriage has shifted to the 'relationship' pattern, reflected in Chapter Five of this book. His analysis of the problem of indissolubility does not assume or depend on conscious or unconscious reservations of one or both of the parties at the time of their marriage. He argues (*op.cit*.: 28):

> Indissolubility is something which has to be brought into being *within the marriage itself.* When they marry, a couple do not suddenly find themselves tied by am indissoluble bond which has an existence independent of them. When they marry, they give their pledge that they will form an indissoluble union of persons through their love for each other. The indissolubility of their marriage is *a task to be undertaken.*

My own approach in this book is different. I completely accept Kelly's 'relationship' analysis, based on our current understanding of marriage that owes a great deal to psychiatrists like the late Jack Dominian. But the solution suggested below is still based on the 'contract' paradigm. The result is the same, whichever the paradigm invoked: in contemporary

Western societies nothing prevents the Church from recognising the dissolution of a marriage that has manifestly failed, offering the rites of the Church for re-marriage, and allowing access to the Eucharist.

Attention was drawn above to an inevitable consequence of the widespread use of divorce in modern Western societies to end a marriage under civil law and open the way to re-marriage. Very rare will be the couple so ignorant of the society they live in that they do not have at the back of their minds the knowledge that in the event of marital disaster they can end the marriage. But proving the invalidity of the marriage contract in most cases is virtually impossible. This suggests that the institutional church should recognise a presumption, when a marriage has manifestly failed, that it was invalid at the start. This might put many canon lawyers out of business, but it would open the door to a completely new approach to Christian marriage, one that emphasises the responsibility of the community and the extended family to support married couples at all stages in their lives, to express the love required by the Second Great Commandment, and to treat them with justice.

There is nothing very novel about this solution. In the later Dark Ages and early Middle Ages the institutional Church was quite ready to presume that the overwhelming majority of the population were 'free' to marry, notwithstanding the seven degrees rule. But close to 100% of all marriages **must** have been invalid under those rules. It was just not practicable to do for millions of peasants and artisans what was ultimately demanded for royal and noble families, that they should carry out extensive genealogical research to establish whether they really were free to marry. The fact that royal and noble families eventually had to search far and wide across Europe, to find brides not barred by the seven degrees rule, demonstrates the artificiality of the presumption that the proposed marriage would not be incestuous under the rule. But it did not matter, because the marriages of the peasantry did not matter to the Church. Their marriages having been presumed to be valid, then in the event of a marital breakdown there was nothing the unhappy peasant or his wife could do about it, because they could not **prove** that the marriage had been invalid. This was a convenient situation for the royal and noble families, and for the bishops and abbots who were large landowners. The only parties who could **prove** invalidity were the royal and noble families – and the bishops, when they wanted to make things difficult for the former.

Marriages failing or in danger

The programmes and systems described in Chapter Five are primarily intended to help couples to lead good, fulfilling, happy and productive married lives. They would express the love of Christ's Church for its members, as set out in the Second Great Commandment. But they would also help to identify and help those whose marriages are failing. The Christian community should encourage couples to discuss their problems frankly and in charity, with each other, with their closest relatives and friends. They should not be expected to admit that they are failing by signing up to a marriage guidance or counselling programme before they have used the resources of the programmes and systems arranged for all parents and their families. Stigmatisation as failures is seldom an effective way to resolve marital difficulties, but if professional guidance and counselling is the last resort it should be on an affordable basis.

Marital failure

Despite all the arrangements suggested in Chapter Five there will be many marriages that fail. The task of the Christian community should then be to minimise the hurt and harm caused by the failure of the marriage, above all to the children of the marriage. There should be programmes available to help the couple to end their marital relationship in an ordered and humane way, respecting each other and ensuring that both parents have easy access to their children, and that they meet frequently to discuss them and their needs, particularly after entering into another relationship.

The potential horrors of the step-parent relationship are the subject of much literature. These relationships are often difficult and the Christian community - including Catholic schools - should be particularly alert to signs of neglect and abuse by step-parents.

Admission to the Eucharist

The debate about exclusion from the Eucharist is focused very much on the divorced parent who re-marries. Because of the preoccupation of the clericalised elite with the institutional church's rules about the indissolubility of marriage, little or no attention is given to the real problem: the breakdown of the marriage in the first place. This obsession with the significance of re-marriage takes no account of the responsibilities of the husband and wife for the breakdown of the marriage. Despite the Church's complex system of tribunals it seems that responsibility for the breakdown is not seen as an issue.

However, there is a place for tribunals to consider marriage breakdown. They would have two functions. The first should be to consider the responsibility of husband and wife for the breakdown. The second should be to consider their conduct leading up to the divorce, and subsequently – particularly in relation to their children. What did each of them do in order to minimise the hurt and harm suffered by their children prior to the divorce? What has each of them done for the children since the divorce? Have they treated each other with courtesy? How have they divided the assets and liabilities of the family? What provision has each of them made, financially and in terms of care and attention, for the children after the divorce? Have they honoured their legal and moral commitments to each other since the divorce?

To deal with these questions it would be reasonable for the Bishop to appoint a tribunal, under the chairmanship of a cleric trained for the role, with a jury of married laity who will give their verdicts after hearing the evidence of the couple, of their adolescent and adult children, relatives and friends. The chairman would make it clear that the Church recognises that the marriage had ended. From the date of the divorce until the tribunal has given its verdicts both parties would be expected to refrain from the Eucharist. In the light of its finding of fact the tribunal would refuse or permit admission to the Eucharist, on a conditional basis and subject to review from time to time, particularly after the re-marriage of the parent with custody of the children.

If the tribunal later concluded that one or both of the parents had failed to carry out their legal and moral obligations to each other and to the children, permission to receive Holy Communion could be withdrawn.

There would be no canonical requirement to attend the tribunal, or give evidence. If one (or both) of the couple had behaved very badly during the marriage, and in the run-up to the divorce, it is likely that he or she would not attend. In that case reception of Holy Communion would be in defiance of the Church, and there would be no question of re-marriage with the rites of the Church. And if the tribunal was not satisfied that the moral, caring and financial responsibilities of one or both had not been honoured after the divorce, then again permission to receive Holy Communion would be withheld or withdrawn, and re-marriage with the rites of the Church would be refused. It is likely that in most cases the really guilty party would never be seen in church again, but the innocent party would be warmly welcomed back into the Christian community.

CHAPTER FIVE
RELATIONSHIP EDUCATION, FROM AGE THREE TO OLD AGE

SUMMARY

This chapter focuses on developments needed to ensure that the suggestions made in Chapters Two, Three and Four are effective. It presents relationship education as a continuous process that starts at the dawn of the child's memory and continues into old age.

It begins when the second child, or the child of an aunt, starts to kick in the womb. It continues with the parents' encouragement to play with the new-born brother or sister, to be kind and gentle. As the first child gets older every opportunity is used by the parents to explain the workings of the human body. As children approach puberty parents can provide sex education, supplemented by formal classes in primary school, where boys can be taught by married men (teachers or parents) and girls separately, by married women. This temporary segregation for part of relationship education should not interfere with provision of lessons in human biology in mixed classes.

The hormonal changes that start at puberty should be explained by both teachers and parents. In secondary school both should be stressing that adolescence is a period of storm and stress. Boys should learn about wet dreams and masturbation. Girls should learn about the menstrual cycle.

When gender self-segregation gives way to heterosexual relationships, classes in literature and music should be used to discuss promiscuity and sexual exploitation. In integrated classes adolescents should learn that there is a normal progression from voluntary gender self-segregation through heterosexual friendship to courtship, betrothal and marriage.

P0.arents and teachers should take notice of adolescents making the transition to courtship. When ready, boy and girl friend could formally exchange rings of base metal in the presence of their parents, to mark the start of courtship. They will both know that in this relationship some intimacies are permitted, on a consensual basis, but definitely not sexual intercourse.

When the couple are ready to declare their intention to get married they could exchange rings of (say) silver at a formal betrothal, making public promises – preferably in church, and in the presence of priest or deacon, as well as their parents - to marry each other. From that time sexual intercourse and co-habitation should be accepted and respected – on one specific condition, that effective methods of contraception are used to prevent a conception before they are married. During this – possibly quite long - period of betrothal the couple should be given every encouragement and assistance in making financial and material preparations for their marriage.

When ready to get married the couple should formally announce their engagement and the date of the wedding, and the bridegroom should give the bride a ring that he can reasonably afford.

After marriage, in addition to support from their respective parents, the Church should provide a programme of support and assistance that will continue until all the children have left home, and then assist parents in their future roles as grandparents and great-grandparents. Eventually the latter in their old age should be helped to cope with the trials of disability and dementia.

Introduction

The Extraordinary Synod on the Family and the Ordinary Symod in 2015 face a wide variety of issues and problems. Many of them are discussed briefly in this book, but four sets of them have been singled out for special attention, leading to suggestions that the Synods might consider:

(a) Pre-marital sexual intercourse, co-habiting and promiscuity (in Chapter Two);

(b) The social functions of sexual intercourse in marriage, responsible parenthood and the regulation of births (in Chapter Three);

(c) Marital breakdown, re-marriage and exclusion from the Eucharist (in Chapter Four);

(d) Chapter Six will consider how it came about that the Church found itself in crisis, during the Renaissance, the nineteenth century and in the mid-twentieth, what the causes were, and what steps could be taken to protect the Church from crises in the future.

This present chapter focuses on the developments required to ensure that the suggestions made in Chapters Two, Three and Four are effective. It presents relationship education as a continuous process that starts when a child begins to develop memory, at the age of three or four, and continues until well into old age, encompassing socialisation within the family, nursery, primary and secondary education, further and higher education, formal preparation for marriage, the care of marriage and the family, adult children, and grandchildren, continuing education, retirement activities, and services of the elderly for their adult children, grandchildren, great grandchildren, and voluntary services in the wider community.

PART I. RELATIONSHIP, GENDER AND SEX EDUCATION

This theme links the first three sets of issues and problems, dealt with in Chapters Three, Four and Five, and leads onto the fourth set, dealt with in Chapter Six.

School-centred arguments about the place of sex education and gender relationships tend to have two outcomes. The first is that sex education is generally provided by a badly informed peer group, leaving parents and teachers to pick up the pieces and deal with the consequences. The second is that the celibate leaders of the Latin Rite Catholic Church approach these issues and problems on the basis of a knowledge of the family based exclusively on their own family of orientation, lacking the knowledge of the laity that is based on their own marital sexuality and their own family of procreation.

Seventy years ago it was the experience of many teenagers finishing their secondary education that they knew nothing about sexual reproduction, and very little about gender relationships, particularly if they had been educated in a gender-segregated Catholic school – as required by a Canon Law observed mainly in its breach. They would have had RE lessons from a priest that were all about unexplained 'purity', about immorality and occasions of sin, but without understanding them. Questions about eunuchs were deftly avoided, like those about fornication and adultery

Meanwhile, parents seventy years ago were extremely reluctant to take the initiative, whereas in earlier centuries parents and the local community had few inhibitions. Children would then have seen a dog mounting a bitch, or a bull mounting a heifer, would want an explanation - and get it. The lack of a constructive interest in homilies – as distinct from denunciations and hell-fire sermons – reinforced the reluctance of parents not living in villages and small towns.

An alternative approach

The alternative is an approach that is theologically well-rooted, starting not when the teenager has left school, not when at secondary school, and not at primary school. It starts in the nursery and crèche. Many mothers do it instinctively when a second baby is on the way, or the mother's sister or cousin has a baby coming. Mother or auntie encourages the three or four-year old to feel the foetus kicking in the womb, and tells the child that soon there will be a little brother or sister, or another cousin, to play with, and that great care must be taken of the new baby. 'How did it get there? Daddy (or your uncle) helped Mummy (or your auntie) to start it, just as they helped you (or your cousin) to start'.

So parents can begin sex and relationship education, reflecting that we are all the children of God, made in His image and likeness, the temple of the Holy Spirit, that we must love and respect everyone. When the baby arrives there will be plenty of opportunities to reinforce this idea that we must love and respect everyone else, and move on to the Second Great Commandment that we should love the neighbour who is everyone else, and not just the new baby. Most parents will remonstrate with the older child over roughness, unkindness, telling tales and appropriating the newcomer's toys.

The social environment of these little children is widened when they go to a crèche or playgroup, and other children are invited into the home to play. A little more sex education can be given by drawing attention to their visible biological differences and different modes of urination. If a bully is identified parents can explain how hurtful physical and emotional bullying is to those who witness it and suffer it, and how children who fail to control their aggressive impulses can grow up as nasty people, often without friends. At bath time mothers and fathers can explain a little more about how babies are generated.

This alternative approach of gradually building up knowledge. and an appreciation of the need to respect everyone, can continue throughout primary education. Every opportunity can be used to explain the workings of the human body *pari passu* with the development of respect for others, and how that is related to courtesy and good manners, at home and at school, reflecting our Christian beliefs.

As children approach puberty, in the upper forms of the primary school, and the lowest in the secondary, it seems best for some relationship education, and most formal sex education, to be provided for boys in class by married men, separately from that of girls – provided by married women – so that both boys and girls can ask rather difficult questions without embarrassment. Should the required married man or married woman not be available on the staff a competent parent could be invited to help[19]. This temporary segregation for part of relationship education should not interfere with the provision of lessons in human biology in mixed classes.

---

[19] It is one of the unhappy paradoxes of Catholic education in English convents that the sisters and nuns proved extraordinarily effective in training their pupils in respect for others, in courtesy and good manners, but practically never used that success to go on to provide sex education and gender relationship education for them. The institutional Church's abhorrence of sexuality, it seems, made them unwilling to ask married women to come into the school to provide what they, as celibates with no knowledge of the family of procreation, and the functions of marital sexuality, were unable to provide themselves.

The school head could also ask mothers to inform a designated member of the school staff when her daughter starts menstruating, and when a son starts to have wet dreams. The school could then arrange for small groups of the boys and (separately) the girls to be withdrawn so that a married man or woman on the staff could explain that these are normal - though sometimes disturbing - transitions in the long process during which a baby becomes an adult man or woman.

At secondary school there will, unfortunately, be plenty of occasions when physical bullying by boys and emotional bullying by girls can be frankly discussed both at school and in the home.

The hormonal changes that start at puberty may already have been explained by teachers in the primary school or by parents. But in secondary school both boys and girls should be warned that adolescence is a period of storm and stress – painful for adolescents themselves, for their parents, and for everyone else. They can be told that it is a particularly difficult period for boys and girls who are beginning to take an interest in each other. Teachers and parents can stress the importance of gentleness and good manners in dealing with adolescents of the other gender, and the dangers of loss of self-restraint.

Boys will already have been told that wet dreams are part of the normal process of growing up. At secondary school they can learn more about the functions of the testes in producing sperm, and its storage in the seminal vessical. They can learn how pressure builds up within the latter and creates a hormonal response while they are sleeping, flooding their unconscious minds with sexual thoughts and images, which in turn trigger an ejaculation while they are sleeping.

A married school master can go on to explain how, in the absence of a wet dream, virile boys soon find themselves distracted by sexual thoughts, while they are at school or at home trying to do other things. They can be told that when these distractions become oppressive they can from time to time themselves stimulate an ejaculation by masturbating, relieving themselves for perhaps a week of the thoughts they would otherwise experience. Once condemned by the institutional Church as mortally sinful, masturbation is now viewed very differently by moral theologians[20], though still condemned in the *Catechism of the Catholic Church* and in *Persona Humana*[21].

Similarly, a married school mistress can explain in more detail the menstrual cycle of the adolescent girl, and later its place in married life, and the conception of children.

---

[20] Fagan (1997: 117-119); Winter (2002:xv).

[21] *Declaration on certain questions concerning sexual ethics*, 1975.

Having left behind collective gender self-segregation, some adolescents – particularly males – descend into promiscuity and sexual exploitation, typified by the legends of Don Juan and many others, which can be used in literature and music classes to illustrate one outcome of the onset of puberty, and point to another, the development in most adolescents of a wide range of heterosexual friendships that do not exploit girls and young women.

PART II. MORPHING INTO MARRIAGE: A STEP-WISE APPROACH

This was examined in some detail in Chapter Two, but preparation for it, by the laity and the institutional church, must be seen as an essential part of relationship education both within the secondary school, in further and higher education and in the family. Details of the relationship education required will vary from society to society and culture to culture. The outline offered here focuses on Western societies. Those in Africa, Asia, the Antilles and small islands of Oceania will need an approach that is appropriate to their cultures.

Heterosexual friendship

In Western societies at present parents are generally aware of the way gender relationships develop by stages into marriage. These start with the development of heterosexual friendships, as adolescents and young adults learn about the other gender in a variety of social situations, and learn more about themselves. When they have had a mixed gender education they may find this a very easy and comfortable experience, but when they have emerged from a single gender education they may find it very difficult and unsettling. Perceptive parents and grandparents understand this and try to minimise the awkwardness and embarrassment, encouraging their offspring to get to know as many of the other gender as possible, and to treat them always with respect and gentleness, both physical and emotional.

At secondary school relationship education should match what parents are doing at home, encourage open discussion in gender-mixed classes of the phases through which adolescents pass on their way from puberty to marriage. Teachers should emphasise to their pupils that their parents have had to cope with the same stresses and joys of developing cross-gender relationships, the importance of quiet, relaxed discussions with parents, and avoidance of door-banging tantrums about the appropriate time to go to bed at night.

Courtship

Relationship education in both the family and the school will recognise that there comes a point when a couple focus on each other, cease to search urther for heterosexual friends, and withdraw to some extent from their wider network of friends. This is often signalled in Western societies by a wish to hold each other's hands in public, and for recognition by parents, the extended family and the wider network of friends that they are now boy-friend and girl-friend.

At this stage the only understood – but not necessarily expressed – commitment they make to each other is to refrain from 'two-timing'. In relationship education at school and at home it should be recognised that the concern of both is to get to know the other in a wide variety of social contexts – his home, her home, dining in a restaurant, visits to cinemas and theatres, dancing, meeting each other's relatives, and going for walks, drives, rides and so on. Relationship education would recognise that there is a great deal of talking, and some tentative kissing and intimate touching. It should also recognise that other members of their peer-group – and particularly their other close friends - should stand back and give them the space they need, that a little friendly banter is acceptable, but no hint of jealousy or hurt feelings.

Parents will be worried that kissing and intimate touching may lead to sexual intercourse, and two or three generations ago preachers would have fulminated about occasions of sin and the evil consequences of impurity. But both teachers and parents might instead see courtship as the time when the courting couple should be thanking God for creating the one being courted, when they say their prayers and at Mass. And they might stress that the Second Great Commandment which requires that love for the other also requires a restraint without which the loved one may be grievously hurt or harmed.

Parents and Church leaders might develop some of the social controls that were found in Roman, Greek, Celtic, Frankish and Germanic societies before clericalisation triumphed in the Middle Ages. Among the folkways used to exercise social control of sexual drives in the Dark Ages were rituals to mark entry into the courtship stage. These provide useful models for development in the third millennium. Boyfriend and girlfriend could exchange rings made of a base metal, in the presence of their parents, when they were ready to declare that they now had a steady relationship. And parents – not the clergy – could ask God to bless the rings and those wearing them. Relationship education at school and in the home would make it clear that discreet kissing and intimate touching by mutual consent, were now permissible, but that sexual intercourse was very definitely not.

Courtship might end in tears, and the rings handed back: certainly painful, but not a disaster. Sanctions? None, unless the girl became pregnant, in which case the couple would face the anger of their parents, and the requirements of the State over the maintenance of the child.

Betrothal

Relationship education in secondary school and at home, would stress the significance of the public declaration of the couple that they **intended** to get married, that they **intended** to commit themselves to each other in marriage. In modern Western societies they might find it very difficult to **make** that commitment to marriage for some time, because contemporary culture expects couples to have at the time of marriage the possessions their grandparents only came to enjoy after many years.

Cultural change has imposed on young couples developments - that they have widely accepted - that are delaying marrying and child-bearing well into their thirties. Relationship education at school, in the family and within the institutional church, should encourage adolescents to put to one side the pressures of advertisers and the peer group that demand an expensive wedding – not just a shared meal after the exchange of their vows, but a full day to impress the guests (and horrify their parents), sometimes two days, with costly entertainments, perhaps abroad.

At school, at university and later, couples should be encouraged to face up to the realities of setting up a home after betrothal or marriage, to recognise that once they have publicly declared their intention to marry they should focus on the material and financial preparations for marriage. The couple should have received at secondary school an introduction to the arithmetic of interest rates, credit cards, hire purchase and mortgages. Preparation for marriage should go on to cover the legal formalities of buying a house and arranging a mortgage, and getting a tenancy of rented property. The 'bottom drawer' should contain not just the bride's nighties and underwear but also the savings accounts they are building up to ensure that they will have the money they will need when they set up house together. During marriage preparation they will have learnt of the dangers of using expensive loans to meet the cost of holidays, computers and furniture.

At secondary school the couple should have had some information and advice on the responsibilities of teenagers who undertake baby-sitting and child-minding. During marriage preparation they should learn more about the gestation of babies, their delivery, pre-natal and post-natal care, either from qualified nurses, midwives and health visitors, or from experienced mothers.

Likewise at secondary school, they should also have received a formal education on budgeting for a family, the opening of savings accounts with a bank or other institution - to which the couple could later turn for a mortgage - the dangers of consumer credit, and the disasters facing those who go to pay-day loan companies. They should have been introduced to simple ways of accumulating the material necessities of married and family life, the need to use not just the bottom drawer but many other drawers and cupboards to accumulate the unwanted household linen, curtains, crockery, cutlery, glasses that other members of their two families would otherwise be throwing away, so that they would need to spend less on filling their new home in the immediate aftermath of their wedding.

This relationship education should embrace their families, encouraging them to set aside for their offspring whatever they don't need themselves, and in particular to assess what the two sets of parents can do to help financially in buying or renting accommodation, reminding them that most parents could only afford to help in this way if the couple budgetted for the repayment of what would normally be loans, so that other members of the family, and later the parents themselves, could make use of the same savings.

Despite the efforts of the couple and their respective families to minimise the length of the betrothal, couples in many Western societies now have to wait much longer than they used to, because of the insecurities of contemporary economies, slipping – almost unnoticed by their politicians and banking institutions - into crises that create unemployment and less secure employment. This has led increasing numbers of couples into pre-marital sexual relationships and co-habitation. The institutional church has failed so far to accommodate this as it did in the Dark and Early Middle Ages, a subject discussed in detail in Chapters One and Two when it was argued that betrothal should be recognised as the first stage of marriage.

With the recognition of betrothal as the first stage of marriage, relationship education would have to prepare betrothed couples for the new relationship that would have started with the public announcement of their intention to marry. They would know that their parents, families, the community, and the institutional church would recognise that they had entered the first stage of marriage. Their relationship education would have prepared them to make public promises to each other in the presence of witnesses and a representative of the institutional church (permanent deacon or priest). They would know that they were engaging in an important rite of passage, the ceremony taking place in the church porch, or the church itself, possibly during Mass, when its significance would be explained.

The couple's relationship education, at secondary school or later, would ensure that they, their families and the Christian community, accepted that after formal betrothal sexual intercourse was permitted -

provided that the couple used effective contraception to prevent the conception of a child before their marriage. Preparation for formal betrothal would include separate opportunities for the man and his future bride to seek and get advice from an experienced – and preferably trained - married person, on bedroom manners, the prelude to love-making, and the many alternative positions for sexual embrace.

At the formal betrothal the couple would give each other rings of (say) silver. All would understand that a long period of cohabitation might ensue. The couple, and the community, would understand that if one or the other, or both, decided that there was to be no marriage they would be required to declare this publicly. Provided there was no pregnancy there would be no sanctions other than any sanctions provided for breach of promise in the Civil Law. Canon lawyers would be kept out of it, but in the event of a birth or pregnancy the couple would know that the maintenance provisions of the Civil Law would apply.

Marriage

Marriage care should have begun at primary school, continued through secondary, further and higher education, into courtship and betrothal. Formal marriage preparation should never be given by celibates – either priests or sisters – but by mature laity with experience of successful marriage, and its difficulties. It should cover the courtesies of making love, the couple's responsibility for the size and spacing of their family, and their moral duty to make conscientious decisions about the methods they use to limit or regulate their family.

The couple and the community would know that the future bride would be given an engagement ring once the date of the marriage had been made public. Since their early years in secondary school the couple would have been prepared for married life. But they would also have learned that the Christian community would be supporting them throughout that married life, celebrating their wedding anniversaries, the anniversaries of their children's baptisms, and that the laity in the Church would assist them in an organised way in the upbringing of their children, and expecting them to help other parents who might be either less well-prepared or less competent as spouses and parents.

In the homily at their marriage the couple would be encouraged to see their love-making as the holy communion of husband and wife, analogous to the Holy Communion of the faithful with Christ in the Eucharist. In their pre-marriage preparation they would have been reminded that sexual intercourse in marriage is no longer seen as something they are entitled to under a contract but as a freely offered expression of their love for each other

Parishes or groups of parishes should be encouraged to develop support systems for couples once they are married. If the couple have a kinship network in the area where they get a home, some of their kin should be invited to discuss with other parents and relatives discreet support for the newly married couple.

The couple should likewise be integrated into the support system by being invited to special Masses in the month when they celebrate their wedding anniversary, to celebrate with other couples the baptismal anniversaries of their children, and to take part in mutual baby-sitting and child-minding groups.

The relationship education of the couple would have assured them that the Christian community would help them, when they needed help, would insist that they supported and loved each other, but above all that they should socialise their own children, nurture and care for them, and prepare them for adult life.

The continuing relationship education of married couples would remind them, as their children grow up, of their perceptions of their own parents, families, and the world of adults, when they were growing up. It would help them to understand the perceptions of their children as they in turn become parents and grandparents, and of the mutual obligations in love of the elderly and their offspring.

These systems of support should continue into old age, as grandparents are brought together from time to discuss how they can best help their children and grandchildren. And in turn middle-aged parents could be asked to consider the options for and care during the last few years of their own aged parents, as they find it more difficult to cope within their own homes.

This approach to the continuing relationship education of married couples is a task for the laity, supported by the institutional church, but not directed by it, and that support is best provided by married permanent deacons.

The relationship education of Catholics, from age three or four well into old age, would underpin gender relationships at all the crucial stages of life – infancy, childhood, adolescence, adulthood, courtship, betrothal, marriage, procreation, nurturing and socialising of children, the latter's independence, the grandchildren, and the old age of the grandparents. At all these stages the focus would be on respecting the obligations of the Second Great Commandment, and at all of them the lead would be taken by the laity, but with the support of the institutional church.

CHAPTER SIX
THE CURRENT CRISIS. CAUSES & CURES

SUMMARY

The fundamental cause of the crisis that erupted in 1968, and deepens each year, is cultural lag. The institutions of the Latin Rite Church managed to accommodate social and cultural change quite well in the Dark Ages. But they adapted to the feudalism of the Middle Ages by building up their own power rather than by making functional accommodations. The resulting tensions during the Renaissance had explosive consequences in the Reformation, and failure to accommodate the latter led to the Thirty Years War in the Seventeenth Century.

There was an apparent accommodation at Trent, but it was very limited. In one respect it increased the potential for cultural lag by enhancing the clericalism of the institutional church.

Vatican I further enhanced the tensions by its formal definition of Papal Infallibility without considering the Episcopal College. Creeping infallibility worsened the tensions, its effects aggravated by the new Papal monopoly in the selection of bishops, set out in the 1918 Code of Canon Law.

Pope John XIII's aggiornamento, and Vatican II, greatly reduced the cultural lag. But Pope Paul VI reserved two critical issues, and towards the end of the Council began to pre-empt debates. The bishops gone, the Roman Curia began to undo Vatican II, and continued to do so until the election of Francis Bergoglio.

The success of Ottaviani at the Holy Office in persuading Paul VI to reject the Pontifical Commission's report, and issue the encyclical Humanae Vitae, resulted in uproar in 1968, and its rejection by the faithful. It also destroyed just what Ottaviani wanted to preserve, the Pope's authority, and created a divide between the institutional leadership and the faithful that widened until the resignation of Benedict Ratzinger in 2013.

Meanwhile, in the five decades since the end of Vatican II the pace of social and cultural change has accelerated, particularly in relation to human sexuality, marriage and the family. It also accelerated technologically, so that millions of the laity are discussing Pope and prelates, cardinals and Curia, every day on the internet.

The fundamental weakness that caused and hid cultural lag was clericalism. The clericalisation of the institutional church began under Constantine. It was weakened during the Dark Ages, but its resumption in the early Middle Ages separated the clergy from the laity, and the clergy developed the characteristics of a caste.

What separated the Latin Rite from the Greek Rite and the later Orthodox Churches was the gradual suppression, first of clerical marriage, and then of concubinage in the Latin Rite. Its consequence was that the Latin Rite clergy no longer shared with the laity the main features of their lives – earning a living, finding a spouse, procreating, supporting a family, and nurturing and socialising children.

Trent strengthened clericalism by requiring that boys aspiring to the priesthood were removed from their families at puberty, and educated in boarding schools where all the pupils were preparing for a life socially separated from the laity.

After Trent the different orientations of clergy and laity were accentuated, the former to the First Great Commandment and 'churchy' things, and the latter to the Second Great Commandment and the struggle to support themselves and their families.

Six features of the institutional culture of the Church underpin clericalism:

- *(a) Narcissism,*
- *(b) Obedience,*
- *(c) Structural sin,*
- *(d) Secrecy and the suppression of the truth,*
- *(e) Orientation to the Great Commandments,*
- *(f) Absence of dialogue with the laity, and*
- *(g) Lack of significant lay participation in the institutional Church.*

The Annuario Pontificio and the Statistical Yearbook of the Church provide massive evidence of the narcissism of Popes and prelates in general, and many of the minor clergy. This narcissism is also strongly linked to clerical paedophilia and the episcopal tradition of covering it up and protecting paedophile clergy.

The emphasis on obedience makes it a test of loyalty. As in many authoritarian regimes the requirement of obedience – of priest to bishop, and bishop to pope – undermines the duty of obedience to conscience. It explains what many in the laity see as the moral cowardice of bishops since Humanae Vitae in failing to challenge it when the laity – and many of the clergy – did so on a massive scale, then failed to challenge the veto on the use of condoms to prevent the spread of HIV/AIDS, the marginalisation of women in the Church, and other issues.

Pope John Paul II offered the concept of structural sin to condemn the lust for power and the desire for profit. It is also a useful tool for the analysis of the lust for power in the institutional Church. Theologians, social psychologists and sociologists have all explained the dysfunctional implications of obedience in relation to conscience. Pope John Paul II overlooked these in his presentation of structural sin in Reconciliatio et

Paenitentia (1984) and Sollicitudo Rei Socialis (1987). In the latter he wrote of fear or the conspiracy of silence' and 'secret complicity or indifference', without apparently recognising how endemic secrecy, forgeries and fraud have been in the institutional Church for a millennium and a half.

The respective orientations of the clericalised elite and the laity to the Great Commandments are very different. The clerics are interested above all in 'churchy' things – worship, liturgy, ritual, the finer points of theology, church buildings, their decoration and vestments. This is a consequence of their orientation to the First Great Commandment. They do not share the laity's preoccupation with earning an honest living and bringing up children, supporting, nurturing and socialising them. The laity often find it difficult to express their love of God, and usually do so by heeding the Second Great Commandment. They do not share the clerics' preoccupation with 'churchy' things.

Bishops often express their wish for dialogue with the laity, but go to extraordinary lengths to ensure that there is only a downward monologue, from themselves to the faithful. As a result, national pastoral councils are rare. Where diocesan pastoral councils exist they often operate in a straightjacket of secrecy and anonymity. Dialogue with the laity at continental and world level is almost non-existent. Gradually, the very effective independent lay-led organisations of the Lay Apostolate, and aid to the Third World, have been castrated by compulsory incorporation into episcopal bureaucracies or the Roman Curia.

The ultimate remedy for cultural lag in the institutional church is de-clericalisation. Ten developments are proposed to bring this about:

(a) Decentralisation;
(b) Opening the priesthood to permanent deacons, whether married or not;
(c) Deliberate efforts to reduce social distance between the clericalised leadership and the laity, and reduction of the social isolation of bishops and clergy;
(d) Creation of a system of public accountability;
(e) Adoption of openness and transparency as norms of the Church, as opposed to secrecy and the suppression of truth;
(f) Development of consultation and dialogue with the laity;
(g) Institutionalisation of consultation of the laity;
(h) Inclusion of laymen, laywomen and women religious in Church government and administration, at all levels;
(i) Opening the diaconate to women;
(j) Reform of the status and roles of women in the Church: a twenty-first centuryAggiornamento;
(k) Public recognition of the roles and contributions of women in

the life and work of the Church;

(l) Encyclical on the historic abuse, denigration & marginalisation of women in the Church, and

(m) Encyclical on marriage, including a proclamation of marriage as a State of Perfection.

These would include the election, at continental level, of six laymen, six laywomen, and six women religious, for appointment to the College of Cardinals, and another six of each elected to meet at least once a year to review the work of each of the departments of the Roman Curia.

Corresponding elections of laymen, laywomen and women religious would ensure dialogue with bishops and officials in the continental episcopal conferences, national episcopal conferences, and dioceses.

An encyclical letter, reviewing the most important (and outrageous) statements made by theologians and popes about women over almost two millennia, and apologising for them, would open the door to allowing women honoured and functional status and roles in the Church.

PART I. CULTURAL LAG AS THE MAIN CAUSE.

The nature of cultural lag

When there is no change in a social system, eg its culture, social structure and economy, or when the change is so slow as to be imperceptible, there is no functional need for other parts of the social system to change – though they might change as a result of changes in the natural environment. This seems to have been the situation of many pre-modern societies.

However when change is fast enough to be perceptible it can gradually build up tensions within the social system. And the faster the change the greater the tensions. The institutional church seems to have dealt with this quite well during the Dark Ages, when social and cultural change resulting from the massive migrations of Germanic and Frankish tribes and clans destroyed the Roman Empire in the West. It not only developed accommodations with the invaders but also demonstrated to them that their own security would be enhanced by their elites' adoption of Christianity. So the Church effectively 'civilised' the invaders.

The emergence of cultural lag in the West

Having civilised the invaders, the institutional church in the Middle Ages greatly increased its authority[22]. The Donation of Pepin in 755,

[22] Here defined, following Weber, as power that is accepted as legitimate, as distinguished from tyranny, power not accepted as legitimate.

confirmed by Charlemagne, gave the Papacy territorial power over what remained as the Papal States until 1870.

Charlemagne's coronation by Leo III in 800 increased the authority of the Papacy in the long term in two ways. First it was no longer subject to the Byzantine Emperor, and second, it allowed later Popes to claim that the Pope's coronation of the Holy Roman Emperor gave him divine authority over the Emperor, and all other rulers. This authority was greatly increased by Hildebrand, and demonstrated by the humiliation of the Emperor at Canossa. It enabled the Papacy to revive the right of the clergy, granted by Constantine, to exemption from the criminal courts. In addition to transferring a great deal of property and treasure to the institutional church, in 318 and 333 Constantine transferred criminal jurisdiction to the bishops, and in 321 and 323 further extended the rights of the clergy (Palanque, Bardy & de Labriolle (1950: 61). As a result, when Becket was murdered by four knights of Henry II, the king was subjected to a humiliating whipping by the monks of Canterbury. In England the Anglican clergy enjoyed the residue of these rights until they were abolished by Acts of Parliament in 1823 and 1827.

While the Latin Rite institutional church in the West was consolidating its power, social and cultural change accelerated during the Middle Ages. Agricultural technology across the West was greatly improved by the monasteries, which also institutionalised education, the care of the sick and social welfare. Improved communications and economic migration spread industrial technologies, and increased the volume of international trade based on comparative advantage. Nation states emerged, with more effective systems of government and law, strong enough to resist invaders from the East, if not the South-East. The re-discovery of the classical Greek and Roman texts - via Christian translators in Syria, the Islamic conquest of Spain, and then the visits of Catholic scholars to Toledo - laid the foundations of the Renaissance. In the later Middle Ages better and more numerous schools greatly increased literacy and broadened the education of large numbers. And the development of universities gave access to higher education for future elites.

It cannot be said that the institutional church was unaware of these changes: many of them it initiated, promoted and supported. However, many of the results of these changes, in the fields of emergent science, theology and political philosophy, were vigorously attacked, so that large numbers were imprisoned, tortured and burnt at the stake. Accommodations like those made in the Dark Ages were not made, so that many in the educated and political elites were brought to the point of revolt.

The Reformation: a consequence of failure to recognise the implications of cultural lag

The Reformation of the sixteenth century split Christianity for the second time. It created havoc in the sixteenth and seventeenth centuries, as hundreds of thousands died in wars of religion, and millions eventually had to emigrate from their homelands. Millions more had to yield to force and accept a politically imposed religion. Most of their descendants found the strain of practising their beliefs intolerable, so that in some countries Catholics, and the adherents of different Churches of the Reformation, survived only in small pockets, living in constant fear of penalties, arrest, or worse.

At Trent the institutional church underlined its refusal to accommodate the social and cultural change of the Renaissance. Its definition of marriage as a sacrament defied the views of both Lutherans and Calvinists. Its condemnation of use of the vernacular for translations of the Bible, and in the liturgy, gravely impeded Christian education and worship. These, and much more at Trent, hardened the split in Western Christianity. This split did not even begin to heal until Vatican II embraced the Reformation doctrine of the People of God, rejected the doctrine of *extra ecclesiam nulla salus,* joined – four and a half centuries late – the Churches of the Reformation in endorsing the use of the vernacular, and expounded a new understanding of the functions of sexuality in marriage.

Trent did effect a measure of accommodation to social and cultural change. For example, it reformed the training of the secular clergy. But, as will be argued below, this accentuated the very weakness in the social structure of the Church that led to cultural lag in the first place, i.e. clericalism and the institutional structures created to strengthen and protect clericalism.

Vatican I: further failure reinforces cultural lag

This Council of the Church is remembered for one development, the formal definition of Papal Infallibility. It is not remembered for its decisions on episcopal collegiality because the new nation state, Italy, ended eleven centuries of the Papacy's civil power, and the Council wound up its work and dispersed without considering the episcopate.

The failure of any European state to protect the Papacy in 1871 meant that henceforth, willingly or otherwise, the Papacy had to deal with states by seeking their compliance by normative means[23]. A century later it appreciated that getting the compliance of the member states of the United

[23] For an analysis of kinds of power and kinds of involvement, leading to a typology of compliance relations, see Etzioni (1961: 3-22).

Nations with its teaching on contraceptives would be very difficult – so difficult that Pope John XXIII took the unprecedented step of setting up an expert Commission of three priests and three lay experts.

In another way Vatican I reinforced cultural lag. A century of 'creeping infallibility' changed the relationship between the Roman Curia and the rest of the Church. Every statement of a Pope, or from one of the *dicasteri*, was received with new attention and respect. Some of these, like the *Syllabus of Errors*, and the condemnation of Modernism, were treated by many as infallible statements, resulting in manifest embarrassment at Vatican II.

Another major factor in the centralisation of power was the assumption by the Papacy, in the half-century after Vatican I, of virtually all episcopal appointments, opening the door to the homogenisation of theological opinion in the episcopate, eventually achieved by Pope John Paul II. The power of the Papacy was greatly increased by default after the annexation of the Papal States by Italy in 1870, leaving the Pope to retire to the Vatican in protest. The 'unspoken compromise' followed later, by which the Italian Government relinquished all the powers of nominating bishops in Italy to the Pope. Then in 1905 the separation of Church and State was decreed in France by an anti-clerical Government which then unilaterally dumped all episcopal appointments on to the Pope. The Papal monopoly of all these appointments was completed nearly nineteen hundred years after the death of Jesus by the 1918 Code of Canon Law (Winter, 2002: 38 & 144-5; Winter, 2014: 26-7 & 45-7). The implications of this unprecedented concentration of thousands of appointments all over the world in the hands of one man will be discussed later

Vatican II: a great effort to reduce cultural lag

There was widespread agreement among many theologians with the views of most religious sociologists that when Pope John XXIII was elected the Church was suffering from massive cultural lag. But few in the Roman Curia had any suspicion that he would soon ask the bishops of the Western Church to join him in undertaking an *aggiornamento.*

In the period between the announcement and the opening of the Council there was a pronounced relaxation of the strict controls over what the clergy wrote in books and journals – via the *nihil obstat* and *imprimatur.* Soon the laity and the clergy alike were able to read in the Catholic press what would have been rejected out of hand a few years earlier. And theologians, especially religious, who had been silenced by the Holy Office were once more able to publish their views, so that the bishops who so wished could consider their opinions before going to Rome.

At Vatican II the Latin Rite bishops had the unusual experience of meeting and listening to the bishops of the Oriental Rites of the Catholic

Church, leading Churches where the secular clergy shared the same life experiences as the laity. They had another novel experience – listening to what their own *periti* had to say - and their *periti* were often very ready to consult the laity, and to heed what they said. There was, moreover, a great deal of openness about the proceedings. The spokesmen of national hierarchies were very ready to give detailed accounts at press conferences of the debates in St Peter's, while individual bishops found many ways of expounding their views in public.

Cultural lag since Vatican II

As a result, over four sessions the Council was able to remedy much of the cultural lag that had accumulated before the Reformation, between Trent and Vatican I, and between Vatican I and Vatican II. Its ability to do so was, however, curtailed in two ways. First, Pope Paul VI reserved to himself the critical issues of the celibacy of the secular clergy and the morality of contraception. And second, he began to pre-empt the debates on some matters. So the *aggiornamento* desired by Pope John XXIII was in no way complete in 1965 when the bishops finally went home.

However, it soon became clear that under Pope Paul VI the Roman Curia was re-asserting the power it had lost in the first few days of the Council when it had been challenged by a number of 'progresssive' cardinals. At the Holy Office Ottaviani succeeded in wresting control of the Pontifical Commission from the Secretariat of State. Then, a few days after the Commission's report, approved by fifteen cardinals and bishops, had been delivered to the Pope by Cardinal Doepfner, Ottaviani went to him and presented what was in effect Father Ford's paper insisting that *Casti Connubii* was irreformable[24].

There followed two years during which Ottaviani at the Holy Office put constant pressure on the Pope to reject the Commission's report, on the grounds that its acceptance would gravely weaken the authority of the Church's institutional leadership. He eventually persuaded Paul VI to accept the draft Father Lio had tabled at the Commission – and which had been rejected - as the basis for the encyclical *Humanae Vitae.*

When *Humanae Vitae* was published in 1968 a marked contrast was quickly apparent between the reactions of the faithful, the People of God, and those of their bishops. The overwhelming rejection of the encyclical by the laity, and many of the clergy, contrasted with the reactions of bishops and Episcopal Conferences. These ran from endorsement - because they agreed wholeheartedly with it - to relief - because the matter had now been settled by the Pope, *Roma locuta est, causa finita est* – then

---

[24] It is curious that no copy of the working papers that underpinned *Casti Connubii* could be found in the Vatican archives.

to some expressions of pastoral concern, and finally to 'pastoral solutions' - such as 'just carry on, don't ask and don't tell'. It seems that not a single Episcopal Conference requested an Extraordinary Synod to discuss the issue[25].

After a century during which bishops had been both selected and appointed by the Papacy - selection having been taken out of the hands of those who had for a millennium and a half selected them, and only then sought Papal ratification – they soon forgot the collegiality they had proclaimed at Vatican II and knuckled down, some gladly, some reluctantly, some timidly, and some in the expectation of promotion – auxiliary to ordinary, ordinary to archbishop, and archbishop to cardinal (Kaufman, *op.cit., passim*). All were aware that their oath of 'loyalty' to the Pope really meant unquestioning 'obedience' .After 1978 it became quite clear that the indispensable criterion for consideration as a potential bishop was endorsement of *Humanae Vitae* (Winter, 2014: 46-8).

The Roman Curia has made little secret of its determination to remedy the 'errors' of Vatican II, and to reinstate the *status quo ante*. On one issue after another discussion has been forbidden, theologians in the priesthood have had to appreciate that there are many matters that they should not discuss, general superiors of religious orders have been required to sanction members whose teaching and published work displeased the CDF, and individual religious theologians have subjected to the most appalling punishments (Kelly, 1992: 138-159).

Meanwhile bishops whose personal conduct was condemned as 'inappropriate', like Jacques Gaillot of Evreux, and Tom Morris of Toowoomba - both refused an audience with the Pope - were dismissed without due process. Archbishop Bezak was similarly dismissed in 2012 because he was raising issues over false accounting, and was then 'barred from speaking to the media'. Another bishop whose personal conduct was even more 'inappropriate' – using public transport instead of his episcopal car, living alone in a flat, cooking his own meals, and wearing old shoes – managed to escape dismissal, and was elected to the See of Rome, where his personal conduct has continued to be 'inappropriate'.

Unfortunately, over the five decades since the end of Vatican II the pace of social and cultural change has not diminished: it has continued to speed up., particularly in relation to human sexuality, marriage and the family. As a result there is in 2014 another massive cultural lag to add to problems not attended to in the late Middle Ages, during the Renaissance, at Trent, at Vatican I and at Vatican II. Over a millennium the institutional church has failed to find a way of recognising cultural lag, and

[25] Kaufman (1995: 90-102)

accommodating it in a manner that respects the values and promotes the mission that Christ gave the Church.

PART II. FUNDAMENTAL WEAKNESSES THAT HID AND CAUSED CULTURAL LAG

Clericalisation and Clericalism

It seems that clericalisation began under Constantine, and in particular with his exemption of the clergy from the criminal justice system of the Roman Empire. This, and the resumption of clericalism in the early Middle Ages, separated the clergy from the laity. The clergy developed the characteristics of a caste[26].

Earlier, men had been selected by the laity to preside over celebration of the Eucharist. Their fellow Christians had recommended them to the bishop for ordination. Once ordained they were subject to some constraints – they were not at liberty to absent themselves for long periods – but they shared with those who had elected them the ordinary roles of the layman. They had to work in order to support their families; they married a wife who would conceive and give birth to children, nurture them, and with her priest-husband would socialise them in preparation for adult life and roles. The bishop-husband too had similar responsibilities to wife and children. And he too had to cope with some constraints. For example he was not allowed to marry again if his wife died – a major constraint when many a married men re-married after the death of a wife (frequently in childbirth) in order that the new wife could nurture and raise his children.

In these circumstances bishop and priest shared the life experiences of the majority of their people. It would not have been necessary for lay couples to explain to bishops and priests – as the lay couples had to when the Pontifical Commission was taking evidence – the functions of marital sexuality; from their own experience they would know, just as the secular clergy of the Catholic Oriental Rites know today.

However, if the clergy were to maintain such privileges as the exemption that Constantine gave them from criminal jurisdiction, and the other 'benefits of clergy', they had in the long run to stress their social distance from the laity, their social boundary. One way to do this was to discourage marriage for the clergy, then to forbid it, then to sanction those who nonetheless got married, later to forbid concubinage and then to sanction priests who kept concubines[27].

---

[26] Wills (2000: 132-150); Winter (2014: 94-156, *passim)* and Winter (2002: 2009-222, *passim.*)

[27] The author's great uncle was a secular priest in Wales before the Great War. He kept a concubine (his housekeeper) who gave him three children, and whom he married when he left

During the Dark Ages the institutional church lost most of its power, and found it necessary over and over again to forbid clerical marriage and to denounce concubinage. When it began to regain its power in the early Middle Ages it still proved unable to control the sexual inclinations of its secular clergy. Worse, the religious orders too – especially the monastic orders – found control of the sexual drive very difficult. This was to be just about the only non-spurious justification for Henry VIII's Suppression of the Monasteries.

During the sixteenth century the Lutheran and Calvinist Reformers rejected any requirement of celibacy before or after ordination. The social status, privileges and social distance of the clerical elite was maintained in the Church of England by other means, despite the freedom of its clergy to marry if they wished.

There have been many different justifications of compulsory celibacy in the Latin Rite Church. Official explanations have often focussed on the need for the priest to be completely at the service of the faithful, but sometimes some stress has been placed on the economic advantages of not having to find the resources to support wife and children as well as the priest himself. During the later Middle Ages, the Renaissance, and afterwards, when cardinals, bishops and senior priests enjoyed lifestyles that most of the laity could not imagine, this explanation was not very persuasive. Looking at the luxurious lifestyles of many bishops and priests today many of the laity still find it so.

Another rationale[28] was the tradition of ritual purity inherited from some pagan societies. This did not require abstinence in the Orthodox Churches because they required Mass to be said only on Sundays. But the celibacy rule antedated the practice of daily Mass in the Latin Rite.

A further rationale had some merit in the lawless Dark Ages. Property given to support a parish might be claimed by the children of a priest as belonging to the family, not to the parish. With the restoration of functioning legal systems in the Middle Ages, just when the celibacy rules were being enforced once more, and the Church's courts were becoming powerful, this justification lost its validity.

Trent exacerbated the clericalism of the institutional church. It did so by its prescriptions for the education of priests. As so many had been very badly educated, reform was very necessary. But it had the result that it separated the priestly caste from the laity at a much earlier age, when they entered junior seminaries. From that time onwards they were labelled as

---

the priesthood. On many occasions in the 1960s I heard - while in clerical company - tales and jokes about priests and bishops who had concubines. Over the next five decades I heard of many fatherless children and adults whose very affectionate and supportive 'uncles' were Latin Rite priests. See also Wills (2000: 187).

[28] Winter (2002: 107-114) and Wills (1973: 104-131 and 133).).

future priests. They were much less influenced by the experience of family life, and at both minor and major seminary their peers were all heading for the priesthood, and kept socially distant from the laity. The implications of these reforms for narcissism and paedophilia are discussed below

Trent's confirmation that the language of the clerics, Latin, was the only language permitted in the scriptures and liturgy of the Latin Rite, in defiance of the adoption of the vernacular by the Churches of the Reformation, deepened the social distance between the majority of the laity who knew little or no Latin and the clerics who did. Within a century few of even the well-educated laity knew a little Latin, and by the time the bishops arrived in Rome in 1962 for Vatican II it was clear that many of them too had difficulty in either speaking good Latin, or understanding those who could not speak it, but tried to.

Since Vatican II the minor seminaries have disappeared. Many future priests have not entered major seminaries until after completing university studies, and often bring to their work as priests an understanding of intellectual disciplines other than philosophy and theology. Considerable numbers have spent some time earning a living, and holding down a job. For real 'late' vocations, who spend only a couple of years in a seminary, the priest may have worked in the 'real world' for a decade or two. And some will have married, been bereaved and then taken up a priestly vocation. Despite 'shortages' of priests today, many are given leave of absence for further studies, so that the educational and professional qualifications of most of the secular clergy today are far superior to those in the 1960s.

In Anglophone countries the secular priesthood now includes considerable numbers of married clergy, formerly Anglican, who have wives, children and grandchildren. Recently, to these have been added numbers of married former Anglican clergy in the Ordinariate. All these, and the permanent diaconate of mainly married men, have demonstrated an ability to bring to homilies and private discussions an understanding of the functions of marital sexuality, of the stresses of getting and holding a job, and nurturing and socialising children and adolescents, that celibate priests cannot.

In short, despite the developments noted above, we have to ask: how is it that the institutional leadership of the Church is now, once more, in very serious cultural lag, out of touch with the real world that it should be evangelising? The effects of compulsory celibacy in the Latin Rite, despite the married former Anglicans and the permanent diaconate, continue to underpin the caste-like character of the secular clergy.

In the Orthodox Churches, the Churches of the Reformation and the Oriental Rite Catholic Churches priests share the main life cycle experiences of the adult laity. Apart from those in some of the less developed countries, adult men – and increasingly women – get training for a career or higher education when they end their education at school. They seek a job, and hold it down. They court a wife, and marry. They procreate, they sustain their marriage, socialise and support their children, and in turn help them to train for a job and find a career. When their own offspring reproduce they help them and the grandchildren. Their expectations of life continue to rise so that in old age one of the couple is likely to be caring for or nursing the other.

This life-cycle experience of married men is not shared by the Latin Rite secular priest, whether or not he gets episcopal ordination. So priests and bishops have personal experience of the family of orientation, as objects of the love, care and attention of their biological parents, but very few have any personal experience whatever of the family of procreation, and of the functions of sexuality in marriage.

Concomitants of clericalism

Six features of the institutional culture of the Church underpin clericalism:

(a) Narcissism,
(b) Obedience,
(c) Structural sin,
(d) Secrecy and the suppression of the truth,
(e) Orientation to the Great Commandments;
(f) Absence of dialogue with the laity, and
(g) Lack of significant lay participation in the institutional Church.

Narcissism

This feature pervades the clericalism within the Church. Popes, cardinals, bishops – and many if not most priests - are fascinated by themselves. The visual evidence is everywhere, of cardinals and bishops in their canonical robes – on the covers of diocesan directories and the pages of Catholic papers.

The 2011 edition of the *Statistical Yearbook of the Church* (published in 2013) devotes 110 pages to statistics of bishops, priests, permanent deacons and other male religious. It provides 60 pages on ecclesiastical territories, and 79 on tribunals. Women religious (of pontifical jurisdiction only) get 30 pages. There are 31 pages on the religious practice of the laity, thirteen on welfare institutions, and ten on educational institutions. So a total of 249 pages are devoted to the institutional world of the clerical males, 30 to institutes of women religious controlled by the Roman Curia, and a total of 54 about the laity and the institutions to support them. Out of 333 pages of statistics 75% are about the male clergy and religious, 9% about the largest institutes of women religious, and 16% about the laity who constitute c.98-99% of the People of God.

The most astonishing aspect of the *Statistical Yearbook* is what it does not include. There are no statistics about Mass attendance. Nor are there any in the *Annuario Pontificio*, despite all the institutional emphasis on Mass attendance.

What the *Annuario Pontificio* and the *Statistical Yearbook of the Church* reveal above all is just the extent of narcissism in the male institutional Church. The clerics are focused on themselves, not on the mission that Christ gave to his Church, nor on the People of God that they are supposed to serve. They are not interested in dialogue with the laity, because they see themselves as 'the Church'. Their own God-given role they see as requiring them to address a monologue to the laity. They see it as the God-given role of the laity to heed that monologue, and obey their commands – 'to pray, to pay, and to obey'.

Three editions of *Rene*w (168-170) contain four articles about clerical paedophilia. In the first Lomes (2013: 168/7-8) focuses on the long history of paedophilia in Latin Rite Catholicism, starting with the *Didache* in the first century AD, then the Synod of Elvira, c.300-309 AD, and then Peter Damian's *Book of Gomorrah*, 1051.

In the same edition Sipe (2013: 168/12-13) distinguishes between 'normal narcissism' and 'acquired situational narcissism'. He argues that there is a

> normal and necessary condition of narcissism at the infantile level of personality development. It is self-evident that most cultures go to great lengths to foster children, keep them safe as they develop a sense of self-worth based on the solid experiences [that] I am loved – I am loveable. The self-centred supports necessary to secure a firm personality are transient and give way to maturing socialization where sharing and the sense that I can love develops as the child matures .

Sipe goes on to discuss 'acquired situational narcissism', to explain the valuation of institutional image over the protection of children.

> Part of the process of introduction into the institution involves a relinquishing to one degree or another of one's self to a circumscribed, all male authority, regulated, supposedly sexually abstinent group where conformity of mind and will are demanded and prized. These are 'total institutions' which confer an alternative identity and security in exchange for the personal sacrifice.

Sipe looks at 'institutional malignant marcissm, the term coined by Kernberg in 1970:

> He pointed out that the psychopath was fundamentally narcissistic and without morality. Malignant narcissism includes a sadistic element, creating, in essence, a sadistic psychopath. The revelations about the sexual abuse of minors and how the institution produces and protects clergy abusers from the highest echelons on down betray the actual social construct of the Church.

Benkert, (2014: 169/4) made the same link between paedophilia and narcissism:

> Many of the priests who abused my patients or that I evaluated are psychosexually and socially immature. They pick immature and vulnerable victims and inject themselves into their lives without concern for harmful effects. They function in an atmosphere of unbridled underdevelopment where they operate above laws and do not have to live with the consequences of their behaviour. They consider themselves special and entitled. One priest admitted to having twenty-two young women sexual partners without thought or concern for the welfare of any of them. Another priest admitted to sexually abusing three hundred young people, mostly boys. Their lack of empathy was startling. Frequently clergy abusers reassure their victims that they are demonstrating 'God's love' in their very act of violation.
>
> This arrogance, self-centredness, sense of entitlement, exploitation, lack of empathy for victims, and rejection of responsibility for destructive behaviours demonstrated in the distorted sexuality of so many Catholic clergy reveals their formation in a culture that can only be identified as narcissistic ….
>
> The all-male secret clerical culture combined with the exclusion and devaluation of women and children form the perfect setting for a flourishing institutional pathological narcissism.

Doyle, a canon lawyer, (2014: 170/4-5) focuses on the training of priests as the source of the narcissism that underpins paedophilia

> Young men training for the priesthood are enmeshed in the clerical world from the very beginning of priestly formation. The seminary environment is an all-male, homosocial enclave in which the sharp distinctions of the clerical social structure are made even sharper as the young men learn that in order to survive they must do the equivalent of surrendering their individuality to the corporate identity, blending in and avoiding any creative thinking. They are taught that bishops are, among other things, the Church's

> ‘official teachers’ which means that they have the final say on the meaning of any Church teaching from mundane matters to the so-called essential truths of the faith.

Upon ordination, Doyle continues:

> The young cleric’s world changes dramatically. He is given what he has been taught are the awesome powers of the priest. He is now admitted to the inner circle of the sacred clerical world, a world that depends for its survival on the exalted and mystical theology of the priesthood but also upon a veil of secrecy that protects the clerical world This dimension tends to reinforce narcissism and strip the cleric of empathy.

None will argue that these observations about paedophilia apply to the secular clergy as a whole, most of whom are horrified by it. But some of these comments can justly be applied to some of the priests who are not paedophiles but whose behaviour illustrates the ‘arrogance, self-centredness, sense of entitlement’ and narcissism described above. It was illustrated in Chapter One in the unguarded comments of two priests and a bishop during the discussions of the Pontifical Commission.

Obedience

The institutional church places huge emphasis on what it declares to be the duty of obedience – of the laity to priests, of priests to their bishop, and of bishops to the Pope (described as ‘loyalty’). It is said to follow from Christ’s teaching and to be based on the authority (i.e. power accepted as legitimate) that he gave to his apostles and to their successors[29].

There are some problems with this approach[30]. They can be illustrated by the world’s experience with Hitler and the Nazi Party. Hitler took great care to ensure his legitimacy as German Chancellor. The Nazi party did not get a majority in the Reichstag in 1933, but they were the largest party. And they had enough support from other parties to secure Hitler’s election as Chancellor. (The numbers of Catholics who supported him swelled massively after the *Anschluss* in 1938.) Having secured a majority in the Reichstag he asked it to cede total power to him, and then dissolve itself. It did so by majority vote, and his opponents were arrested as soon as they left the building, and thrown into concentration camps.

Milgram’s experimental work[31] demonstrated that when ordinary people are instructed by an authority to do something that they are morally

[29] Winter (2002: 125-152, *passim*); Winter (2014: 116-156: *passim*); Spencer (2014, *passim*)
[30] Fagan, 1997: 89-111); Winter (2002: 125-152, and 2014: 116-156).
[31] Milgram (1997: *passim*).

anxious about they will continue to obey for a long time before they finally disobey. Not only the SS but ordinary German soldiers obeyed orders without protest. It is not remarkable that two men who later became Popes - Karol Wojtyla and Joseph Ratzinger - obeyed the orders of the Nazi regime until the very end of the war. What is remarkable is that one simple laymen, Jaegerstaetter, impelled by his conscience, refused to the last, and suffered execution by the regime[32].

The matter of personal conscience is central to this issue of obedience to authority. Sereny's interviews [33] with senior Nazis demonstrated their persistent unwillingness to admit any wrong-doing or error. This is another feature of the Roman Curia over a millennium. The victim is expected to wait centuries for anything like an apology, and after being burnt at the stake an apology does not really seem adequate. Fagan's writings on conscience and sin[34] have led to the imposition on him of appalling sanctions by the CDF, but for many of the laity they have clarified the operations of conscience. In particular they contest the views of so many institutional leaders that an 'informed' conscience means a conscience that conforms to their own views – always presented as 'the teaching of the Church'. Instead he argues that the conscience must be 'informed' about the nature and circumstances of matter: one cannot properly make a moral decision without taking the trouble to consider the motives of the participants and the circumstances. This obliges us to consider the use of secrecy by the institutional church, and its readiness to suppress the truth

Few would compare the Pope with Hitler, or the Roman Curia and the bishops with the Nazi Party. But the illustration does suggest that it is not sufficient that the power of the leadership is accepted as legitimate. The exercise of power must pass other tests. It must be seen as reasonable and conducive to the common good. It must respect the dignity and rights of those whom God created in His own image and likeness. It must respect other norms, such as those set out in International Law, be proportionate, and so on. And Christians might point to the Second Great Commandment.

Given these tests of the **exercise** of power it is very difficult indeed to defend the record of large numbers of Popes and bishops over the last millennium and a half. In daily life we take the duty of obedience to authority for granted: we stop at the traffic lights when they turn red, we reluctantly pay our taxes, teachers order, and sometimes get, silence in class. Life would be incredibly difficult if we had to examine our consciences about the hundreds of commands we get each day, and decide which we should obey and which we should disobey. But most of us, from time to

[32] Zahn, 1967: 177-196).

[33] Sereny (1983: *passim*; 1995: *passim*).

[34] Fagan (1988: *passim*) and (1997: *passim*).

time, are faced with a command that does trouble our consciences. And the commands of the institutional leadership of the Church are often very troubling indeed.

In recent decades several writers[35] have given detailed attention to the moral issue of obedience to the commands of legitimate leaders, as a result of the Nuremberg Tribunal set up after the War to try war criminals. At that Tribunal the excuse that 'I was just following orders' was utterly rejected. Senior military officers ever since have not been able to claim that they were acting on the orders of president or prime minister. Private soldiers can no longer plead that they were just carrying out the orders of a junior officer. Unfortunately, this is another instance of cultural lag in the institutional Church, whose leaders continue to demand obedience from laity who are rather better informed about what kinds of orders ought to be obeyed, on moral or ethical grounds, and what should be disobeyed.

Sipe (2013: 168/13) observes that

> as a man moves up in the ecclesiastical system, more conformity and obedience are expected and demanded for further advancement Obedience that binds an individuals (even blindly) to authority is the ultimate test of loyalty, and proof that the individual can now justly assume institutional identity. There is little psychic distinction between self and institution and thus one's value is subsumed by identification with the power, prestige, and status of the church. Clerical dress advertises the identity, and elaborate public ceremony that dignifies prelates in impressive rich robes adds to the attraction to identify with the whole church institution, suffused with its power, arrogance, vanity, and inordinate self-esteem.

In his discussion of institutional malignant narcissism Sipe argues:

> Sociopaths, those without empathy and conscience, flourish in the institutional atmosphere of the Roman Catholic clerical system. Obedience, not charity or justice, is the guiding principle within the clerical structure. In the centre of the vow cardinals take before the pope is the phrase: I vow to keep secret anything confided to me that if revealed would cause harm or scandal to the Church. The blind obedience to authority (the pope) extolled and inculcated in clerics on every level of the institution kills the development of spirituality. It distorts conscience because truth is

[35] Stanley Milgram (1974), Michael Winter (2014), Gita Sereny (1974 and 1995), Sean Fagan (1997: 112-132), Spencer (2014: *passim*).

subservient to the institutional mind that is dedicated primarily to self-preservation at all costs. A lie is not a lie if spoken according to institutional values.

So we have had, until the election of Francis Bergoglio, three types of response to commands within the Church. Bishops have generally obeyed the commands of the Roman Curia, whatever they think about them. Secular priests have sometimes complied because they had no reason to disobey, and sometimes quietly failed to comply, on conscientious grounds. Some secular priests, and numbers of religious priests, have taken a stand, and have been disciplined – or worse. Most of the laity comply when they can accept the commands in good conscience, and disobey them when they cannot.

The difficulty with these responses is that the cultural lag worsens. Because national Episcopal Conferences failed over forty-five years to challenge *Humanae Vitae* it remains a running sore. Because they failed to challenge the Roman Curia and the Pope over the ordination of married men, the use of condoms to prevent the spread of HIV/AIDS, the status of women in the Church, and so on, nothing was done. While sociologists have an understanding of the very positive functions of conflict, the institutional leadership sees it as entirely dysfunctional. Bishops and national Episcopal Conferences do not seem to understand the concept of 'the Loyal Opposition', even in countries where political parties and electorates recognise that the contest between government and opposition is the key to the successful working of democratic political systems.

Structural sin

The embryonic concept of structural sin was intended by Pope John Paul II[36] to castigate the wicked world and its lust for power and riches. But it was almost tailor-made to illuminate developments in the Church's culture and institutional structure, particularly since 1870, that have wreaked havoc on the Church, particularly in Latin Rite Catholicism. He completely ignored the critical role of obedience to authority in his very useful concept of structural sin. In a footnote to *Sollicitudo Rei Socialis* the Pope wrote:

> Whenever the Church speaks of situations of sin, or when she condemns as social sins or the collective behaviour of certain social groups, big or small, or even of whole nations, or even of whole nations and blocs of nations, she knows and she proclaims that such cases of social sin are the result of the accumulation and

[36] In *Sollicitudo Rei Socialis (1987)* and *Reconciliatio et Paenitentia (1984)*. It seems curious that Winter (2002 and 2014), Fagan (1997) and Kelly (1992) do not consider structural sin.

concentration of many personal sins. It is a case of the very personal sins of those who cause or support evil or who exploit it; of those who are in a position to avoid, eliminate or at least limit certain evils, but who fail to do so out of laziness, fear or the conspiracy of silence, through secret complicity or indifference; of those who take refuge in the supposed impossibility of changing the world, and also of those who sidestep the effort and sacrifice required, producing spurious reasons of a higher order. The real responsibility, then, lies with individuals. A situation – or likewise an institution, a structure, society itself is not in itself the subject of moral acts. Hence a situation cannot itself be good or bad.

It is most improbable that the Pope was reflecting on the treatment of the Pontifical Commission on Births, of the Commission's report, and its subsequent rejection, though these fit his account of structural sin. It is also most improbable that he was reflecting on the emergent scandal of clerical paedophilia, though this too fits neatly into his analysis. But fear, conspiracies of silence, secret complicity and indifference were endemic in the institutional church before Vatican II, and since.

The Pope argued:

> 36. .... It is not out of place to speak of 'structures of sin', which are rooted in personal sin, and thus always linked to the concrete acts of individuals who introduce these structures, consolidate them and make them difficult to remove. And thus they grow stronger, spread, and become the source of other sins, and influence people's behaviour.

This statement is quite clear as to the origin of 'structural sin', but it does not explain how sinful acts of an individual become consolidated, 'difficult to remove, grow stronger, spread, become the source of other sins, and so influence people's behaviour'. Yet is a very good summary of the development of clericalism in the Church since Constantine exempted clerics from the criminal jurisdiction of the Roman Empire.

Later the Pope wrote

> 37. ... among the actions and attitudes opposed to the will of God [and] the good of neighbour, and the structures created by them, two are very typical ... the all-consuming desire for profit, and ... the thirst for power, with the intention of imposing one's will upon others ....

This seems a fairly accurate summary of the development of clericalism by the Roman Curia over the last millennium.

Secrecy and the suppression of the truth in the culture of clericalism

Few will dissent from the comments of Pope Paul II about secrecy. They might add, however, that secrecy has been endemic in the Roman Curia for well over a millennium. Even now, four and a half decades after Pope Paul VI was presented with the twelve volumes of evidence submitted to the Pontifical Commission, they remain secret. Important information, both qualitative (reports and papers) and quantitative (statistics and accounts), is routinely treated as secret[37]. Over the centuries this routine practice of treating all information as secret, unless there is a strong and pressing reason to disclose or publish it, has become established at both diocesan and national levels[38].

Pope John Paul II refers inadvertently to another feature of clericalism: the conspiracy of silence. The fraudulent Donation of Constantine legitimated the Pope's control over his territories until the much later – and historically real - Donation of Pepin in 755. In the interval, there was a conspiracy of silence about the authenticity of the Donation of Constantine. And the False Decretals[39] influenced Church policy and practice from c.852 until finally discredited as forgeries in 1628. So the conspiracy of silence of the last century over clerical paedophilia has a long pedigree[40]. So too has the culture of fraudulent behaviour in the financial institutions of the Roman Curia, corrupted by links with the Mafia and Freemasonry, and their use as means of disguising transactions that the secular world will no longer tolerate. And now it is recognised that for decades the powerful heads of some religious orders and movements have been allowed by conspiracies of silence to do whatever they like with the huge sums that have passed through their hands.

Orientations of the clergy and the laity

Finally, another major factor, already noted, separates the priestly caste from the laity: orientation. The former is focussed on 'professional' theological issues that are of very little interest to most of the laity, on the sacramental activities over which they preside, on ritual and the liturgy, churches and chapels and their arrangement and decoration. They can happily spend large sums of parishioners' money on windows to commemorate Canon So-and-So, or yet another statue to Our Lady in yet

---

[37] Spencer (2014). *The suppression of the truth by institutions of the Catholic Church. An essay on the theology, social psychology and sociology of structural sin.* (Awaiting publication).
[38] Winter (2002: 158ff), Winter (2014: *passim*).
[39] These purported to be the decisions of some thirty popes of the first three centuries, supporting the claim of the papacy to temporal as well as spiritual authority. They were actually written in the ninth century (Duby: 291).
[40] Wills (2000: 176-192). See also Lomes (2013: 168/7-8), cited above.

another of her many roles. Bishops likewise have no difficulty in finding and spending huge sums of the laity's money on their latest gimmick[41] without giving any thought to accountability. All this demonstrates an orientation to the First Great Commandment, to love God.

Overwhelmingly, however, the laity are oriented to the Second Great Commandment, to love their neighbour. They do not find it easy to communicate their love of God directly, but can express it indirectly by using the myriad opportunities of everyday life, by respecting the rights and dignity of those they encounter, by being polite, thoughtful, generous, understanding and supportive in what they say and do, and coming to the rescue when someone they encounter seems to be in trouble. They support charities and non-profit agencies, and they do what they can to help their children and grandchildren through higher education, and to help them to acquire a home. And as their own parents and grandparents, and their friends and neighbours, reach old age they are alert to the difficulties and problems they encounter, watch over their safety and try to be helpful and give much time, thought and attention to providing them with a safe, comfortable and enjoyable old age.

Two annual publications, The *Annuario Pontificio* and the *Statistical Yearbook of the Church*, illustrate the different orientations of the clerical elite and the laity, the former towards the First Great Commandment and the latter towards to Second. Both of these annuals are based on the Annual General Statistical Questionnaire. Apart from getting a few figures about educational and welfare institutions the Questionnaire is exclusively concerned with 'Churchy' matters. No one reading the Questionnaire, any more than editions of the *Annuario* and the *Yearbook*, would appreciate that one of the two Great Commandments is 'to love one another as I have loved you'.

This clerical fixation of the Roman Curia on professional 'Churchy' things is matched at national level in the statistics collected by Episcopal Conferences. It is seen in the topics on which figures are collected by the Episcopal Conferences in both the USA and England & Wales. These topics have changed a great deal since the end of the War, but they do not include attention to the Second Great Commandment. Any competent social statistician could devise questions that would reveal a lot about what the People of God are doing – or not doing – to express their

---

[41] In the Archdiocese of Westminster over the calendar years 2002-2005 a total of £2,007,000 was spent on the Cardinal's 'At Your Word, Lord' programme, despite the opposition of his clergy. No evaluation was carried out when the programme ended. When Bishop of Arundel & Brighton he had carried out a similar programme. Again, there was no subsequent evaluation. To the £2 million must be added the costs incurred by parishes, and individual parishioners. I asked one of the latter what difference it had made to her life. She replied: 'I did get to know a few more fellow parishioners'.

love of neighbour. But the bishops who make the decisions are not interested in quantitative expressions of the truth in general – statistics and accounts - and have little interest in what the laity do about the Second Commandment, so long as they do as their bishops command[42].

The absence of dialogue with the laity

The reality is that the laity account for over 98% of the People of God. It is therefore astonishing that dialogue at all levels between the laity and the institutional leadership has not been promoted since Vatican II[43]. It is even more astonishing that so many attempts have been made by the Roman Curia[44], and by national Episcopal Conferences[45], to reduce even further the minimal dialogue that has survived. The clericalisation of the Church is not far short of total.

As already noted, this clerical insistence on top-down monologue instead of dialogue is seen most vividly in two annual publications of the Roman Curia, the *Annuario Pontificio* and the *Statistical Yearbook of the Church.* The 2011 edition of the former names c.28,000 people in its index of names. Out of 410 pages, ten were sampled, listing 693 names. These included forty women religious (mainly Superiors General of the women's institutes of pontifical jurisdiction), two laymen (both *gentiluomini* to the Pope), and no laywomen. The *Annuario* devotes 1,160 pages to clerical institutions which do not name any member of the Church who is neither a priest nor a bishop. However, it must be said that the staff of the Secretariat of State does include significant numbers of laymen and laywomen. And of the 75 named at the Pontifical Council for the Laity, fourteen are cardinals, six bishops, twelve clerics, twenty-four laymen, and nineteen laywomen. Of the 36 named as 'members' of the Council eleven were cardinals, one was a bishop, one a cleric, thirteen were laymen and ten laywomen.

---

[42] The writer drafted the parish register return form introduced by the Catholic Church in England & Wales from 1955. It has been amended many times since then, as a result of decisions of the Roman Curia and the Catholic Bishops Conference of England & Wales. It could seek much more useful information, in particular about lay responses to the Second Great Commandment. Five major reports, in ten years, have recommended improvements. Four were completely ignored. The latest was rejected outright.

[43] Daniel in Hornsby-Smith (1999: 78-98)

[44] Cf the treatment of *Caritas Internationalis*. This was the very effective lay-led international representative body of the various Catholic charitable agencies throughout the world. Until the 2005 edition of the *Annuario Pontificio* it did not appear in its index. Following *Durante l'Ultima Cena*, in September, 2004, it was taken over by *Cor Unum*, to the dismay of Caritas agencies throughout the world.

[45] For the treatment of dialogue in England & Wales see Daniel *loc. cit.* Spencer (2014) chronicles the decline of the National Council for the Lay Apostolate into torpor as a result of its takeover by the Catholic Bishops' Conference of England & Wales that followed *In the House of the Living God* in 1982, and its re-naming as the National Council for Lay Associations. See below.

Lack of significant lay participation in the institutional church

As clericalism has no place for dialogue with the laity it has no need for significant lay participation in the institutional Church. Paradoxically, the Apostolate of the Laity flourished in 'the bad old days' before Vatican II. However, that very effective apostolate, associated with the Jociste Movement, Pax Romana and lay organisations concerned with the Third World, has - as noted above - been castrated by incorporation into the new structures created at both the international level by the Roman Curia, and at national levels by Episcopal Conferences [46]. Very few

[46] At both world level and national level it seems that hitherto excellent lay led Catholic organisations find it increasingly difficult to continue their work of creating Christ's Kingdom on earth once they lose their independence and become creatures of the Church's professional bureaucracy. Their inclusion in the index of the *Annuario Pontificio* usually marks the beginning of their end as effective agencies.

[46] Spencer (2014) exemplifies the consequences of institutional takeover of flourishing lay-led organisations by describing the contents of the website of the National Association of Lay Associations on 12 November, 2012:

The website of the National Association of Lay Associations now reveals[46] that:

- Access is restricted
- Visitors to the site can read and download its 2003 Annual Report (but not earlier or later reports)
- Visitors can also read about CAFOD's ideas about celebrating the 40th Anniversary of *Populorum Progressio* in 2007
- The Newman Association's entry had been up-dated as recently as 25 October, 2012
- The National Board of Catholic Women entry offers its *Newsletter* of October, 2012
- The National Justice & Peace Network offers its 2012 conference report, focussed on China
- The Catholic People's Weeks offers its programme for 2012, last up-dated on 25 April, 2012
- The Catholic Association for Racial Justice offers an advert for Racial Justice Sunday, 9 September, 2012
- The Catholic Students' Council website "cannot be found"
- The Catholic Men's Society sites either cannot be found or cannot be displayed
- The Volunteer Missionary Movement site "cannot be displayed"
- The Society of St Vincent de Paul site is entirely in Spanish
- The other fourteen member associations of the NCLA are not even named, nor are the eleven liaison representatives
- The website offers tips for writing a letter to your MP: a December, 2003, letter to Patricia Hewitt, UK support for peace in Sudan, and a letter to the BBC re Popetown)
- For questions and comments visitors can click sam@ncla.org.uk But Sam Corcoran had left the NCLA long ago
- The website does not name any of its five officers and five advisers

countries have a National Pastoral Council. Where no National Pastoral Council exists few dioceses seem to have a Diocesan Pastoral Council. And the few that do exist seem to operate in secrecy, with dioceses providing little information about them, their members and their activities.

A further major problem is the lack of relevant published qualitative and quantitative information already referred to. Institutional leaders understand very well that knowledge is power, and having no intention of sharing power with the laity they ensure that relevant knowledge is withheld from the laity, and from most of the clergy.

PART III. CULTURAL AND STRUCTURAL REMEDIES FOR CULTURAL LAG

The immensity of the problems facing the two Synods

With fundamental problems going back a millennium and a half it is quite unrealistic to expect either the Extraordinary Synod on the Family in 2014 or the full synod in 2015 to resolve them all. They will require many Synods or a General Council, and - as the decades that have passed since Vatican II have demonstrated - a Roman Curia determined to block the implementation of the work of a Council is able to do so unless its power is checked and its culture is radically changed. Even if the Extraordinary Synod and the 2015 synod were to attempt to deal with all the issues set out in this book it would take a great deal of time to make decisions, work out their implications, apply them in practice and persuade institutional leaders to embrace them.

However, it is not unreasonable to hope that the Extraordinary Synod on the Family and the 2015 synod will select a few issues as being of high priority, and then deal with them, leaving other issues for later consideration.

Priorities

Three sets have already been discussed at some length as being closely related to 'the Family':

(a) Extra-marital sexuality and co-habitation;
(b) Marital sexuality and the regulation of births;
(c) Marriage breakdown and re-marriage after divorce.

Recommendations about these have already been set out. A fourth is given particular attention at the end of this final chapter, i.e.

(d) Aggiornamento in the status and roles of women in the Church.

One more, however, also deserves high priority, as a remedy for the inability of institutional leadership to resolve the above four issues: the de-clericalisation of the Church.

De-clericalisation

Francis Bergoglio is said to be as critical of clericalism as any sociologist of religion[47]. But a structural system that has separated clerics from the laity for a millennium and a half cannot be scrapped overnight: it is too deeply rooted within the Church. What could be done is to take a series of individually small but important steps that would ameliorate clericalism:

(a) Decentralisation;

(b) Opening the priesthood to permanent deacons, whether married or not;

(c) Deliberate efforts to reduce social distance between the clerical elite and the laity;

(d) Creation of a system of public accountability;

(e) Adoption of openness and transparency as norms of the Church, as opposed to secrecy and the suppression of truth;

(f) Development of consultation and dialogue with the laity;

(g) Institutionalisation of consultation of the laity;

(h) Inclusion of laymen, laywomen and women religious in Church government and administration, at all levels;

(i) Opening the diaconate to women;

(j) Status and roles of women in the Church: a twenty-first century *aggiornamento*;

(k) Public recognition of the roles and contributions of women in the life and work of the Church;

(l) Encyclical on the historic abuse, denigration & marginalisation of women in the Church;

(m) Encyclical on marriage, including a proclamation of marriage

---

[47] In para. 102 of *Evangelii Gaudium*, when discussing 'Other ecclesial challenges', he writes: Lay people are, put simply, the vast majority of the people of God. The minority – ordained ministers – are at their service. There has been a growing awareness of the identity and mission of the laity in the Church. We can count on many lay persons, although still not nearly enough, who have a deeply-rooted sense of community and great fidelity to the tasks of charity, catechesis and the celebration of the faith. At the same time, a clear awareness of this responsibility of the laity, grounded in their baptism and confirmation, does not appear in the same way in all places. In some cases, it is because lay persons have not been given the formation needed to take on important responsibilities. *In others, it is because in their particular Churches room has not been made for them to speak and to act, due to an excessive clericalism which keeps them away from decision-making.* (My italics).
This seems to express an extremely limited view of clericalism in the institutional church, and gives no hint as to what Francis Bergoglio plans to do about it. The italicised sentence is taken from one of 288 long paragraphs in the Apostolic Exhortation.

as a State of Perfection;

Decentralisation

Prior to Constantine the Latin Rite Church survived because it was very decentralised. But that had important dysfunctions. In particular it facilitated the emergence and development of a variety of Christian theologies, at a time when theological disputes could do great damage to both emergent Christianity and civil order.

Constantine greatly facilitated centralisation within the Church. But the *Volkerwanderung* came near to destroying the Papacy. The Latin Rite Church survived in southern, western, northern and central Europe because it rediscovered its early decentralisation, as local bishops made local accommodations with migrating or invading tribes and clans, leaving the Papacy with the role of protecting theological orthodoxy.

In different parts of Europe, as the Dark Ages gradually gave way to feudalism the Papacy began to reassert its old central control, through repressing simony, the Investitures Struggle, and marital rigorism (Kaufman, 1995: 174-179). Eventually compromises acceptable to Church and State were developed, lasting until the Reformation. After Trent the institutional church had to adjust to a new situation. Large parts of Europe rejected Catholicism, and the Papacy could exercise influence at best. Even in Catholic countries, like France under Louis XIV, the Papacy could be in major conflict with the State, and its control over the bishops greatly attenuated. In the Americas, Africa, Asia and Oceania, distance and the religious colour of the local political regime made central control impossible.

All this changed in 1870. First, the Papacy no longer had to exercise civil control over the erstwhile Papal States. It could concentrate on extending its control over the institutional church. Second, its power to do so was greatly enhanced by a fortuitous consequence of the loss of the Papal States. The Italian Government had no wish to nominate the bishops to the numerous Italian dioceses. By the 'Unspoken Compromise' all episcopal appointments in Italy were handed over to the Pope.

Third, another fortuitous event, the formal separation of Church and State by the anti-clerical French Government in 1905 resulted in the Papacy getting the patronage of all the French dioceses. The process was completed by the 1918 Code of Canon Law. For the first time in almost nineteen centuries the Pope had the unfettered right to nominate bishops to every diocese in the world, and could dismiss a bishop without due process. This was a personal decision of the Pope himself, not made by an Ecumenical Council.

Fourth, developments in communications technology – telephones, radio, TV, and the internet – enabled the Papacy to follow in detail the activities of any bishop in the world, to communicate quickly, and to receive from third parties information about the bishops' deeds and misdeeds. It gave the Papacy a not dissimilar ability to keep an eye on, and get information about, priests aspiring to episcopal ordination.

These developments have led to the creation of an episcopate of 'yes men', particularly since 1978 (Winter, 2014: 22-59, *passim*); Kaufman (1995: 148-173, *passim*). Bishops who dissent keep their thoughts to themselves, and once retired they publish them in an interesting book. Meanwhile, they are always at risk of being denounced by means of anonymous e-mails. In many ways they are treated by the Papacy like district managers of a supermarket chain: head office gives them orders, and their duty is to obey. But there is one important distinction: they have no right to due process, and no right to appeal to the civil courts against wrongful dismissal, whereas the district supermarket manager has both.

The developments described above flout the principle of episcopal collegiality set out in *Lumen Gentium*, and the principle of subsidiarity set out by Pope Pius XI in *Quadrigesimo Anno* in 1931. The leadership of the institutional church in general, and the Papacy in particular, have a remarkable penchant for expounding general principles for all other institutions to follow, and then ignoring their application within the institutional church (Kaufman, 1995: 152-3; Winter, 2002: 36-7 and 68)[48].

De-centralisation within the institutional church, taking both episcopal collegiality and the principle of subsidiarity seriously, would begin to weaken clericalism by exposing clerics to the laity who live in the real world and not the 'churchy' world of the clerical elite.

Opening the priesthood to permanent deacons, whether married or not

At present permanent deacons straddle the clerical elite. They are part of it, and in Anglophone countries are 'Reverend'. But most of them are married, and almost all of them have been and are financially independent of the institutional church. In these respects they are still part of the laity, and are so perceived by the laity. Their ordination as secular priests would go further in demolishing the wall that has for so long separated the clerical elite from the laity. Their ordination would bring the clerical elite at both diocesan and parochial levels into regular contact with men who would then be *de jure* priests while continuing *de facto* to share the life experiences of the laity.

---

[48]Examples abound. Despite many centuries of denouncing homosexuality the institutional church at Trent prescribed the creation of seminaries that were likely to attract boys and men with homosexual inclinations, where the staff included homosexuals, and then ordained many who were homosexual (Wills, 193: 204). *Divini Illius Magistri* in 1939 proscribed coeducation in general in stringent terms, but dioceses had opened, were opening and continued to open such schools. Pope John Paul II condemned 'structures of sin' in civil society, but they abound within the institutional church.

Their ordination would strengthen the Church in another way. In countries – particularly in some parts of Latin America - where there is already a desperate shortage of priests, the ordination of *viri probati* would permit millions of the laity who now seldom have the opportunity to hear Mass and receive the Eucharist to do both regularly.

Deliberate efforts to reduce the social distance between the clerical elite and the laity

The loneliness of the secular clergy has been largely unremarked for generations, if not centuries[49]. It is justified on many pseudo-theological grounds, but it is extremely dysfunctional. Senior clerics living in great comfort in Rome have been either unaware of it or unconcerned. As bishop, archbishop and cardinal, Francis Bergoglio was very aware of the public perception of bishops and cardinals living like the prince-bishops of the Renaissance, and so he chose to live in a flat and cook for himself[50]. But it seems that by the time he was elected Bishop of Rome he had come to understand the dangers of loneliness and social isolation. So the next step in his long unfinished personal pilgrimage was to move into the *Domus Mariae,* where he could enjoy the company of priests visiting Rome.

This is a model that could and should be used throughout the Church, allowing the bishop to enjoy the company of others, but without the daily responsibilities of domestic governance that an abbot would have. And there is no reason why the company the bishop gets should be confined to clerics. Laymen – and women – should likewise be found sharing his table.

The other side of the coin is that the laity should not feel inhibited from asking the bishop in turn to accept their hospitality and company, not at magnificent receptions but in their homes[51]. This could become a regular feature of visitations, when the chairman/woman of the parochial pastoral council would invite the bishop, the parish priest and the other officers of the pastoral council, to join the family for a meal, and meet their children and grandchildren.

---

[49] The author's mother was perhaps exceptional. During the War she made a point of asking the parish priest to supper from time to time. The author was a civil servant living in digs in the late 1950s. Just before going home for Christmas with his family he went to the PP to wish him a happy Christmas, remarking: 'I expect you will be flooded with invitations over Christmas'. He replied: 'When I have said my third Mass I will go straight to bed, and I won't see a soul until after Christmas'.

[50] Cf Winter (1985: 109).

[51] During the 1950s and 1960s I was invited to lunch on separate occasions with two diocesan bishops, an archbishop and the whole episcopate of a small country. I never had the opportunity to return the compliment. I know of only one couple who have invited a cardinal to supper.

Such customs are much more needed for the parochial clergy, to alleviate their loneliness and enable them to get to know their own parishioners. Just as families take it in turn to take the altar-breads and wine to the altar at the offertory, they could and should take it in turn to ask the parish clergy to join them for a meal and recreation. A former President of the Royal College of Psychiatrists, Sheila Hollins (2010: 7) suggested that the laity could do more to support the clergy with friendship. Citing a study of predictors of better mental health, she argued that one of the five things we all need is a daily hug[52]. Dominian (1975:154) insisted that the community

> will have increasingly little appreciation for the priest as the one who remains the outsider and acts from a distance. This key notion of the priesthood as the man apart has *no* future.

Later (*loc.cit.*: 159) he argued that

> the relationship of priest and people must pursue a much greater closeness than has been the habit for centuries.

However, the Second Great Commandment and the psycho-social needs of the last half century are not the only reasons for taking steps to break down the social barrier between the clerical elite and the laity. The analysis of narcissism outlined above makes it essential to promote social as well as functional interaction between the clerical elite and the laity.

There is a fundamental irony in this proposal to reduce the social distance between the clerical elite and the laity. This distance did not come about by accident. Lawrence (1975: 138-146) shows how celibacy in the Latin Rite priesthood was introduced in the fourth century, and gradually enforced over the next millennium. As late as the thirteenth century married priests and concubinage were still taken for granted by the laity in rural areas. The social distance created by celibacy was deliberately accentuated in the Middle Ages by the enforcement of celibacy in the Latin Rite priesthood (Duby, 1984: 116). And it was then deliberately reinforced by Trent.

---

[52] As an altar boy during the War, who frequently consulted Fortescue's *Ceremonies of the Roman Rite Described*, I was intrigued by the *solita oscula* at High Mass. At least the institutional church allowed priests a very formal hug. One of the most successful and significant innovations since Vatican II has been the 'Sign of Peace' at Mass, when for a minute everyone turns to all around, smiles, shakes hands, or (as I do) kisses wife, daughters and grandchildren. The gesture goes back to the second century (Francis, *Tablet*, 9062, 18. Aug., 2014: 6). How extraordinary it is then that, with the Bishop of Rome daily demonstrating similar human warmth, that the Congregation for Divine Worship and the Discipline of the Sacraments urges more 'sobriety' on Massgoers, and requires the celebrant to remain in the sanctuary.

Creation of a system of public accountability

The institutional church shares with the Chinese Communist Party, some of the successor states of the Soviet Union, and miscellaneous autocratic regimes across the world, a self-view that denies any need to account to those it serves for the resources it gets and uses, for the outcomes of its programmes – in effect for what it actually does. Annually the institutional church does publish *L'Attivita della Sante Sede* and the *Statistical Yearbook of the Church*. Neither of these is remotely comparable to the documents that are published annually by the United Nations and its many agencies - or to those that are taken for granted in the West and in many countries that have embraced democracy and the values of the Enlightenment. Failure to account truthfully and fully for government and governance is heavily criticised, as is failure to live up to expectations.

This self-exemption from the public accountability that is required of major political, economic, social and cultural institutions gradually led to a situation so embroiled in corruption and misgovernment that Benedict Ratzinger recognised that he had to go, and leave to his successor the cleaning out of the Augean Stables. Journalists have noted that there is no world in Italian for 'accountability', just the vague word *responsabilita*, which means something rather different.

Had the institutional church embraced public accountability after Vatican II most of the problems discussed in this paper would have been resolved, and the Church would not have suffered massive alienation. Fifty years later, the institutional leadership of the Church will not recover the confidence of either the People of God or of the world community if it does not establish effective public accountability, within the Roman Curia, national Episcopal Conferences, dioceses and parishes.

Adoption of openness and transparency as norms of the Church, as opposed to secrecy and the suppression of truth

Clericalism has been sustained, protected and extended by the withholding of both qualitative and quantitative information. This has done enormous damage to the mission that Christ gave the Church. The culture of secrecy has been so strong that it has often undermined major plans of the institutional leadership itself[53].

---

[53] In 1958 Cardinal Marcello Mimmi, Secretary of the Sacred Congregation of the Consistory, and the member of the Roman Curia responsible for emigration, wrote to Cardinal D'Alton, Archbishop of Armagh and Primate of All Ireland, to suggest that the British and Irish Hierarchies should agree 'a detailed plan to address the pastoral needs of Irish emigrants in Britain, which should be based on a detailed statistical study of Irish emigrants, including their occupations, destinations and methods of expatriation'. In September 1959 Cardinal Mimmi addressed the Fourth National Congress of Diocesan Delegates for Emigration in Spain and suggested that 'Had all the Irish people, who have emigrated to England throughout the

It has never been explained how secrecy and the suppression of the truth can be reconciled with the moral obligation to tell the truth[54]. As part of the clerical culture of the Catholic Church it goes back to the Donation of Constantine, and has continued ever since. Perhaps the Synods might demonstrate a little repentance by asking Francis Bergoglio to publish the twelve volumes of papers of the Pontifical Commission. More important is the development of a new culture within the institutional church, reflecting that of the democratic societies of the West - and many other countries - where both secrecy and the publication of papers, statistics and accounts are governed by well-known and respected norms[55].

Development of consultation and dialogue with the laity

In the democratic societies of the West it has been taken for granted for a century or two that effective government depends on consultation with those likely to be affected by legislation, government plans and programmes. Before Vatican II this was never accepted by the

---

centuries, kept their faith, perhaps the number of Catholics in the latter country would be twelve million instead of the three million they now number'. Shortly afterwards the International Catholic Migration Commission in Geneva asked the Newman Demographic Survey (NDS) in London to prepare for its Congress in Ottawa in August, 1960, a report on *Arrangements for the integration of Irish immigrants in England and Wales*. The first draft of the report, still lacking the final chapter, was circulated to those who had contributed information. It was rejected in the strongest terms by Archbishop McQuaid in Dublin. After weeks of fruitless negotiations over the text it became clear that a text acceptable to Dr McQuaid and the NDS could not be ready in time for the congress in Ottawa. The unfinished draft report had to be sent o the ICMC to be locked in its safe, and neither published not publicised.

Along with many other NDS reports – unpublished because of a general bar on publication not removed until 2005 – the report for the ICMC remained in the NDS archives. Most of the draft text was discovered by a distinguished Irish historian in the archives of the Archdiocese of Dublin. It was eventually published by the Irish Manuscripts Commission in 2012. It had never been disclosed to either the Irish or the English Hierarchy, or to either the Irish or British Governments. It had therefore no impact whatever on the 'arrangements'. The intentions of the responsible cardinal in the Roman Curia, and a greatly respected international Catholic organisation, were completely frustrated by what was in fact a conspiracy between Cardinal Godfrey and Archbishop McQuaid to ensure that the report was never published. Godfrey's motive was diplomatic: English dioceses were heavily dependent on Irish priests. McQuaid's motive was public relations.

[54] For a discussion of truth and truthfulness, see Winter (2002: 153-168). It has to be said that the institutional church is probably little worse than political parties in suppressing the truth. As this book was readied for the printer the English media were full of details of the way local politicians, civil servants and police in Rotherham suppressed information about the sexual abuse of 1,400 girls by UK-born men of Pakistani origin. However, politicians do not put truth at the top of their hierarchy of values, while Catholic bishops claim that they do.

[55] All the annual Catholic school census reports for England and Wales, for the years 1992 to 2006, were withheld from publication, and still are. When, after many critical reports on this secrecy, some of the data was published for 2007 and later years, the most important statistics continued to be withheld.

clerical elite, and it has not been since that Council ended in 1965. Lip service to dialogue is given occasionally by bishops and Episcopal Conferences, but it seldom materialises. The clerical elite prefer to address what they believe to be the problems without consulting the laity – and seldom even the priesthood – untroubled by their very different perceptions of the problems.

Unless the Synods of 2014 and 2015 can change the clerical culture of the Church, so that consultation becomes a normal feature of the Church's work in carrying out the mission Christ gave it, cultural lag will not just continue but will accelerate – because social and cultural change in the world continues to accelerate. Clerics cannot stop it. If they cannot, will not or do not consult the laity – who are aware of rapid social change in their everyday lives - all they can do is put their heads in the sand.

This failure to consult is matched by a consistent failure to respond to the laity when they are bold enough to take the initiative in the hope of creating the dialogue. At all levels from the Roman Curia to the Episcopal Conference, to the diocese and the parish, letters can be written year after year without a response. Sometimes there is a reply from the Episcopal Conference or the diocese, but it is usually just a polite acknowledgement or expression of thanks for the letter (which enclosed a report, paper or memorandum). The castrated lay organisations of the once flourishing independent Lay Apostolate are similarly unresponsive now that they have been swallowed up by the ecclesiastical bureaucracy[56].

Institutionalisation of consultation of the laity

Consultation and dialogue require institutions. Instead of developing institutions for dialogue after Vatican II the clerical elite resisted requests that they be created[57]. When the institutions for dialogue already existed, as a result of lay initiatives, they were often deprived of their independence, stifled, and became moribund.

The institutionalisation of dialogue is needed at all levels, from Roman Curia to parish. If it is undertaken in the expectation that it can be controlled it will not succeed. Institutions created to facilitate dialogue with the institutional leadership have to be both independent of the clerical elite and dependent on those they represent. When laity are dependent financially on the clerical elite they become prisoners of those who pay their salaries; they become 'yes men', telling their paymasters what they want to hear. And if they are not linked, by election or nomination, to their constituency,

[56] In 1982 the vigorous National Council for the Lay Apostolate in England and Wales was taken over by the Episcopal Conference, and became the National Council of Lay Associations. See Daniel (1999: 78-98).
[57] Hornsby-Smith (1987: 37-41).

but are employed as professional experts, they are extremely vulnerable - unless their professional integrity is institutionally protected[58].

This inevitably leads to consideration of organisational models. The Weber-Rudge typology[59] provides analysis of five models:

(a) Traditional or patriarchal;
(b) Charismatic;
(c) Rational-legal or bureaucratic;
(d) Human relations or democratic; and
(e) Organic or systemic.

Rudge argued that only one of the five was inherently unsuitable for a religious organisation: the rational-legal. But this has been the main model of the Roman Curia since 1870 and seems to have been the principal model of the Episcopal Conferences that emerged in the later 1960s. Its great weaknesses are bad lateral communications, downwards communications limited to commands, and upwards communications limited to 'yessing the boss'. As a result of these weaknesses it cannot easily cope with rapid social and cultural change.

The traditional model was that of Christianity for much of the last millennium and a half. It can only change slowly, so that cultural lag soon emerges, adaptation and accommodation does not happen, or is delayed. So catastrophe can ensue, as it did in the sixteenth century.

The charismatic model is excellent for rapid social change: it was Hitler's model in the 1920s and 1930s. It is the model of many of the great Christian saints, and that of many a mother foundress of a woman's religious order. But it is unpredictable, and when the charismatic dies his or her charisma can quickly be transformed into a tradition that is very resistant to change.

The democratic model is very familiar in the West. It allows plenty of participation and consultation. But it also permits participants to choose their own goals, displacing those of the community or the institution. It is, therefore, a risky model for a Christian Church

The organic or systemic model directs a lot of attention to the environment of the enterprise, and to the social and cultural change taking

---

[58] Early in 1963 the writer was Director of the NDS, and was commissioned by an English diocese to prepare a school planning study. The General Secretary of the Catholic Education Council, the main client of the NDS, did not like the main conclusion of the report, and requested an amendment, but this was refused. A few months later the writer was asked by the Newman Association (NA) to prepare a paper to be read at a Conference of the NA in October. Again the General Secretary of the CEC objected to the draft paper and insisted that the writer should withdraw from the conference, failing which the Bishops would withdraw their support from the NDS. The writer did not withdraw, the paper was read, episcopal support was withdrawn in December, 1963, and the NDS was closed down two months later. The paper was finally published in 2005.

[59] Peter Rudge, *Ministry and Management* (1968: 21-36).

place in that environment. It relies heavily on the well-informed expert, and on having at the top someone who can re-state the objectives of the society or institution so that they are true to its core values but still accommodate rapid social and cultural change in its environment. Pope John XXIII reflected that model, with his desire for *aggiornamento*, his willingness to consult, and to listen to experts. It remains to be seen whether Francis Bergoglio reflects that model, or the charismatic[60].

In the present circumstances it is simply not possible for the two Synods to do more than recommend a few changes in the formal organisation of the Church that might alleviate some of the difficulties that attract so much attention and negative comment at present. Among these is the establishment of pastoral councils for consultation and dialogue, all the way from the parish to the Roman Curia, via the deanery, the diocese, the national Episcopal Conference and the continental Episcopal Conference. The lay members of these pastoral councils should be elected from the tier of councils below, and none should be on the Church's payroll.

The inclusion of laymen, laywomen and women religious in Church government and administration at all levels

There are no theological obstacles to the appointment of laymen, laywomen and women religious to the College of Cardinals. One of each should be elected at continental level, so that at the next conclave there would be at least six laymen, six laywomen and six women religious taking part in the election of the next Pope.

Similarly, there should be six elected laymen, laywomen and women religious appointed to review, at least annually, the work of each of the *dicasteri* (departments) of the Roman Curia. In each case they should receive detailed annual reports, accounts and relevant statistics, and sit alongside the clerics who meet annually to review the work of the department. For example, in addition to the bishops and clerical theologians sitting around the table there would be al least eighteen elected theologians to review annually the work of the Congregation for the Doctrine of the Faith. Similarly, another eighteen would meet annually to review the work of the Pontifical Council 'Cor Unum'.

At continental level there should be elected laymen, laywomen and women religious to sit annually with the bishops, to review the work, annual reports, accounts and statistics of the continental episcopal conference.

[60] For an analysis of the organisational problems of the Church in the late 1960s, using the Weber-Rudge typology, see A.E.C.W Spencer "The Future of the Episcopal and Papal Roles". Pp 63-84 in *IDOC International-North American Edition*, 3 (9 May), 1970, re-published by the Pastoral Research Centre, 2005.

At national level there should be elected laymen, laywomen and women religious to sit annually with the bishops, to review the work of the work, annual report, accounts and statistics of the national episcopal conference, prior to the meeting of the elected national pastoral council.

At diocesan level there should be elected laymen, laywomen and women religious, to sit with the bishop and his chapter to review the work, annual report, accounts and statistics of the diocese, prior to the meeting of the diocesan pastoral council.

It should be a basic principle that at all levels no lay person should be eligible for election if he or she was financially dependent on the institution.

Opening the diaconate to women

The treatment of women by the institutional church is slowly coming to be recognised as scandalous[61]. The Gospels make it clear that it was women among the disciples who had the diaconal, caring, service role. They also showed courage that was somewhat lacking among the male disciples. Later, in Rome, it was again the women who had the diaconal role. And the courage they showed during the persecutions was extraordinary. In the earlier lists of saints women figure prominently.

It is then all the more remarkable that once the process of clericalisation started under Constantine two things happened. Women were confined to the affective, service, caring role, so that they could be excluded from the instrumental role that the male clerics kept for themselves. This was legitimised by references to the patriarchy of Greek and Roman societies, and later of the Celts, the Germans, the Franks and Viking societies. Psychologically, the male elite has over time tried to compensate for the marginalisation of women in general by the adulation and veneration of Our Lady and (when not abusing and denigrating them) putting women onto pedestals (Daly, *op.cit.*:105-123, *passim*). For many centuries when women were difficult they could always be sent to a convent where they could not interfere in the things that mattered.

Yet, despite being confined effectively to the diaconal service role they were overlooked when it came to the status ladder, the bottom step of which was doorkeeper and the top step bishop. Ecclesiastically, the clerical elite had the diaconal **status**, on a temporary basis, while women always had the diaconal **role**.

Opening the diaconal status to women would symbolise recognition by the institutional church that its treatment of women has been disgracefully unchristian. It would also bring women into what is now a male elite, and in doing so would change it. Most women might well be

---

[61] Cf Daly (1968, *passim*), Kelly (1992: 86-103, *passim*) and Wills (2000: 104-121, *passim*.)

appalled at the prospect of becoming part of the clerical elite, but offering women the status of deacon, to go with the role they have had for two millennia, might be seen as the start of de-clericalisation throughout the Church.

Other proposals concerning the roles and status of women in the Church are set out below.

The status and roles of women in the Church: a twenty-first century *aggiornamento*

In recent decades the treatment of the women, who make up half the Church, by the male clerical elite who have dominated it since Constantine, has slowly come to be recognised as scandalous and opposed to fundamental Christian values[62].

The recommendation made above that women be admitted to the permanent diaconate represents one small but significant step in righting a grave and foolish historical wrong. Among others that should be considered are:

(a) The inclusion of laywomen and women religious, as well as laymen, in the bodies that govern and administer the Church, at all levels from the Roman Curia to the parish;
(b) An encyclical, or formal declaration of the synod, apologising for the historic abuse and denigration of women in the Church, and their marginalisation;
(c) Public recognition of the roles and contributions of women, lay and religious, in the work of the Church.

These points are further discussed below.

Public recognition of the roles and contributions of women in the work of the Church

Many of the Churches of the Reformation have done this for a long time. Putting on the glossy cover of the diocesan directory a photo of the elected diocesan president of the Catholic Women's League, instead of the bishop, would remind everyone that almost half of the faithful are lay women.

An encyclical on the historic abuse, denigration and marginalisation of women in the Church

There is a huge amount to apologise for. A good starting point is suggested by a footnote in Blair (1987: 84), commenting on William Birmingham's anthology *What Modern Catholics Think About Birth Control:*

[62] Daly (1968: *passim*); Wills (2000: 104-121, *passim*).

The most shocking contribution in this book was Daniel Sullivan's history of Catholic thinking about women, marriage, love and sexuality. This thinking, wrote Sullivan, has been based, in part, on views expressed by some of the most eminent fathers and doctors of the church: of St Jerome, that a woman is 'the devil's gateway, a dangerous species, a scorpion's dart.' Of St John Damascene that she is a 'sicked she-ass, a hideous tapeworm, the advanced post of hell.' Of St Clement of Alexandria that it 'is shameful for her to think about what nature she has.' Of St Francis de Sales that married couples should not think about the act they might have to perform at night. Of St Thomas Aquinas that 'woman is misbegotten and defective.' Of Pope St Gregory the Great [that] the woman's 'use' is twofold: harlotry or maternity.

The abuse of women, by theologians, popes and prelates over a millennium and a half, has been so widespread that such an encyclical would take quite a time to draft, and would require a great deal of introspection by Catholic theologians about the treatment of women by the celibate male elite.

An encyclical on marriage, including a proclamation of marriage as a State of Perfection

If the two synods are not to be a complete failure they should be followed by an encyclical on marriage,

- abandoning *Casti Connubii* and *Humanae Vitae*,
- recognising the duty of parents to be responsible in their decisions about the number and spacing of their children,
- recognising the right of husband and wife to choose the most appropriate methods to do so,
- recognising betrothal as the first step in marriage,
- recognising the morally licit character of co-habitation and sexual intercourse by betrothed couples,
- recognising that once a marriage has irretrievably failed it is effectively dissolved,
- recognising that re-marriage with the rites of the Church is permissible after divorce,
- recognising that – after due enquiry into the moral culpability of the parties has been concluded – it may be appropriate for one or both to be re-admitted to the Eucharist, and
- recognising the duty of the Church to educate the faithful about human relationships, from early childhood to old age, and to support them throughout their married lives.

It is unlikely that many of the laity know much about the 'Institutes of Perfection'. Those who do may see them as yet another example of the narcissism of the clerical elite. Recognition of marriage as a State of Perfection might be seen by all as an expression of regret for the denigration of marriage over a millennium and a half, and as recognition that in the twenty-first century the institutional church honours marriage, just as it did at Vatican II. It might also encourage those who are married to be good husbands and wives, mothers and fathers.

Given the moral panic about clerical paedophilia and abuse, the concept of Institutes of Perfection might best be quietly forgotten.

SUMMARY OF SUGGESTED SYNODAL RECOMMENDATIONS

BETROTHAL AND CO-HABITATION (Chapter Two)

(a) That betrothal be recognised by the Church as a critically important first stage in the process of getting married;

(b) That the co-habitation of a betrothed couple be recognised by the Church as morally licit; and

(c) That sexual intercourse of a betrothed couple be recognised by the Church as morally licit, subject to their using effective methods of contraception.

SEXUAL INTERCOURSE AND RESPONSIBILITY WITHIN MARRIAGE (Chapter Three)

(a) That the use of contraceptive measures to space and limit births be recognised by the Church as morally licit;

(b) That the choice of contraceptive measures be recognised by the Church as a matter for the couple to decide; and

(c) That the Church reminds couples that they have a duty to act responsibly in deciding the number and spacing of their children.

MARITAL FAILURE, DIVORCE AND RE-MARRIAGE (Chapter Four)

(a) That the Church should remind couples of the damage suffered by the off-spring of a marriage when it fails irretrievably;

(b) That the Church should recognise its collective responsibility

- to sustain and support marriages;
- to ensure that, when a marriage has failed irretrievably, both spouses do all in their power to end it without rancour, and to give over-riding priority to the welfare of their children;

(c) That the irretrievable failure of a marriage should be presumed by the Church, without further enquiry, to be a sign that it was probably invalid at the outset;

(d) That admission to the Eucharist after divorce, and access to the rites of the Church for re-marriage, should be subject to the findings of a tribunal of the local Church on the conduct of the two spouses, before, during and after divorce (and re-marriage).

RELATIONSHIP EDUCATION (Chapter Five)

(a) That the Church should accept responsibility for the relationship education of all the faithful, from age three to old age;

(b) That relationship education should be treated by the Church as a continuous process involving the family, Catholic primary and secondary schools, chaplaincies in further and higher education, parishes and lay Catholic organisations; and

(c) That at marriage the Church should shift its attention from preparation to support and assistance of the couple.

PROTECTING THE CHURCH FROM FUTURE CRISES (Chapter Six)

(a) That the institutional church should recognise that its fundamental problem over a millennium and a half has been cultural lag;

(b) That the institutional church should recognise, as Pope John XXIII did, that the basic cure for cultural lag is continuous *aggiornamento*;

(c) That the institutional church should recognise that the basic cause of cultural lag is clericalism;

(d) That the institutional church should recognise the seven features that underpin clericalism :

- Narcissism;
- Obedience;
- Structural sin;
- Secrecy and the suppression of the truth;
- Orientation to the Great Commandments;
- Absence of dialogue with the laity, and
- Lack of significant lay participation in the institutional church.

(e) That the institutional church should start the process of de-clericalisation by

- Decentralisation;
- Opening the priesthood to permanent deacons, whether married or not;
- Deliberate efforts to reduce the social distance between the clerical elite and the laity;
- Creation of a system of public accountability in the Church;
- Adoption of openness and transparency as norms of the Church;

- Development of consultation and dialogue with the laity;
- Institutionalisation of dialogue and consultation with the laity, and
- Inclusion of laymen, laywomen and women religious in Church government and administration, at all levels;
- Opening the diaconate to women;
- Twenty-first century *aggiornamento* in the status and roles of women in the Church.
- Public recognition of the roles and contributions of women in the life and work of the Church;
- Encyclical on the historic abuse, denigration & marginalisation of women in the Church; and
- Encyclical on marriage, including a proclamation of marriage as a State of Perfection.

(f) That the institutional church should start the institutionalisation of dialogue and consultation with the laity, and *aggiornamento* in the status and roles of women in the Church, by:

- the appointment to the College of Cardinals of at least six laymen, six laywomen and six women religious, all independent and elected at continental level;
- the appointment to each of the departments of the Roman Curia of six laymen, six lay women and six women religious, all independent and elected at continental level, to take part in an annual review of their work;
- the election of similar elected laymen, laywomen and women religious, all independent, to sit with the bishops at least annually to review the work of the continental episcopal conferences;
- the election of similar independent laymen, laywomen and women religious to sit with the bishops of the national episcopal conference, annually, to review its work prior to regular meetings of the elected national pastoral council;
- the election of similar independent laymen, laywomen and women religious to diocesan and parish pastoral councils.

REFERENCES

ABBOTT, Walter M. (Ed.) *The Documents of Vatican II*. London & Dublin: Geoffrey Chapman, 1966.

BENKERT, Marianne. 'Spirituality and the Culture of Narcissism. Pt 2. Clinical observations. *Renew* 169 (March, 2014): 3-4.

BIRMINGHAM, William (ed.). *What Modern Catholics Think About Birth Control.* New York: Signet, 1964.

CATHOLIC BISHOPS CONFERENCE [OF ENGLAND & WALES] . *In the House of the Living God*. 1982.

CATHOLIC CHURCH. *Annuario Pontificio.* Vatican City: Libreria Editrice Vaticana.

CATHOLIC CHURCH. *Durante l'Ultima Cena*. 2004

CATHOLIC CHURCH. Congregation for the Clergy. Directory for the Ministry and Life of Priests. Rome: Libreria Vaticana, 2013.

CENTRAL STATISTICAL OFFICE OF THE CHURCH. *Statistical Yearbook of the Church*. Vatican City: Libreria Editrice Vaticana.

COLLINS, Sheila. 'To whom can priests turn for their daily hug?' *Tablet,* 17 July, 2010.

CONGAR, Yves M. 'Reception as an Ecclesiastical Reality'. *Concilium* 77 (1972): 57-76.

DALY, Mary. *The Church and the Second Sex.* London: Geoffrey Chapman, 1968.

DANIEL, Philip. 'Have we seen the death of dialogue?' Pp. 78-98 in Hornsby-Smith. *Catholics in England, 1950-2000. Historical and Sociological Perspectives.* London & New York: Cassell, 1999

DOYLE, Thomas P. 'Spirituality and the Culture of Narcissism'. Pt 3. *Renew* 170 (June, 2014): 4-5.

DULLES, Avery. 'The Question of Non-Reception'. *America,* Nov., 1986.

DUBY, Georges. *The Knight, the Lady and the Priest*. London: Allen Lane, 1984.

ETZIONI, Amitai. *A Comparative Analysis of Complex Organizations. On Power, Involvement and Their Correlates*. New York: Free Press, 1961.

FAGAN, Sean.

1977. *Has sin changed? A Book on Forgiveness.* Wilmington: Glazier

1997. *Does Morality Change*? Minnesota: Liturgical Press.

FRANCIS BERGOGLIO. *Evangelii Gaudium. Apostolic Exhortation on the Proclamation of the Gospel in Today's World,* 2013.

HOLLINS, Sheila. 'To whom can priests turn for their daily hug? *Tablet,* 17 July, 2010.

HORNSBY-SMITH, Michael P.
1987. *Roman Catholics in England*. Cambridge: CUP.
1999. *Catholics in England, 1950-2000. Historical and Sociological Perspectives.* London & New York: Cassell, 1999.
JOHN PAUL II.
1984. *Reconciliatio et Paenitentia.*
1987. *Sollicitudo Rei Socialis*
KAISER, Robert Blair. *The Encyclical that Never Was. The Story of the Commission on Population, Family and Birth, 1964-66.* London: Sheed & Ward, 1987.
KAUFMAN, Philip. *Why You Can Disagree and Remain a Faithful Catholic.* New York: Crossroads, 1995.
KELLY, Kevin
1982. *Divorce and Second Marriage*. London: Collins.
1992. *New Directions in Moral Theology. The Challenge of Being Human*. London: Geoffrey Chapman.
KUHN, Thomas. *The Structure of Scientific Revolutions.* Chicago: Chicago University Press, 1962
LOMAS, Gabe. 'Paedophilia and the church. The harsh reality.' *Renew* 168 (December, 2013): 7-9.
McClory, Robert. *Turning Point. The Inside Story of the Papal Birth Control Commission and How Humanae Vitae Changed the Life of Patty Crowley and the Future of the Church.* New York: Crossroad, 1995.
MILGRAM, Stanley. *Obedience to Authority. An Experimental View.* London: Pinter & Martin, 1997.
NEWMAN, John Henry. *An Essay on the Development of Christian Doctrine.* New York: Image Books/Doubleday, 1960.
NOONAN, John T.
1957. *The Scholastic Analysis of Usury*. Cambridge, Mass.: Harvard UP.
1965. *Contraception. A History of its Treatment by Catholic Theologians and Canonists.* Cambridge, Mass.: Harvard UP.
PALANQUE, J.R. , G. BARDY and D. de Labriolle. *De la Paix Constantinienne a la Mort de Theodose.* Vol. 3 of FLICHE, Augustin and Victor Martin, *Histoire de l'Eglise*. Paris: Bloud & Gay, 1950.
PAUL VI. *Humanae Vitae,* 1968.
PIUS X, Pope.
1930. *Casti Connubii.*
1939. *Divini Illius Magistri.*

RUDGE, Peter F. *Ministry and Management. The Study of Ecclesiastical Administration.* London: Tavistock, 1968.
SCHILLEBEECKX, E. *Marriage: Secular Reality and Saving Mystery.* Vol II. *Marriage in the History of the Church.* London: Sheed and Ward, 1965.
SERENY, Gitta.
1983. *Into that Darkness. An Examination of Conscience.* London: Random House.
1995. *Albert Speer: his Battle with Truth.* Picador.
SIPE, A.W. Richard. 'Spirituality and the Culture of Narcissism. Pt 1: The Clerical Sub-Culture'. *Renew* 168 (December, 2013): 12-13.
SPENCER, Anthony E.C.W.
1970. 'The Future of the Episcopal and Papal Roles'. IDOC international – North American edition, 3 (9 May): 63-84. Republished, Taunton: Russell-Spencer, 2005.
2010. *Secrecy in the Catholic Church. The Case of Catholic School Statistics in England & Wales.* Taunton: Russell-Spencer.
2012. *Arrangements for the Integration of Irish Immigrants in England and Wales.* Dublin: Irish Manuscripts Commission.
2013. *Statistics, Evangelisation and the Statistics of Evangelisation. A Critical Account of Two Re-organisations of the Pastoral & Demographic Statistics System of the Catholic Church in England & Wales, 1991/2 and 2000/1.* (Unpublished report to the Dept of Evangelisation & Catechesis of the Catholic Bishops Conference of England & Wales).
2014. *The Suppression of the Truth by Institutions of the Catholic Church. An essay on the theology, social psychology and sociology of structural sin.* (Awaiting publication).
UNITED NATIONS. Dept of Social & Economic Affairs.
Demographic Yearbook.
Statistical Yearbook.
WILLS, Garry. *Papal Sin. Structures of Deceit.* New York: Doubleday, 2000.
WINTER, Michael M.
1979. *Mission Resumed?* London: Darton, Longman & Todd.
1985. *Whatever Happened to Vatican II?* London: Sheed & Ward.
2002. *Misguided Morality. Catholic Moral Teaching in the Contemporary Church.* Aldershot: Ashgate
2014. *Recovering Catholicism. An overdue review of the Catholic Church..*
ZAHN, Gordon C. *War, Conscience and Dissent. London:* Geoffrey Chapman, 1967.

SELECT INDEX